# OVERHEARD
# BY GOD

A. D. NUTTALL

# OVERHEARD BY GOD

FICTION AND PRAYER IN

HERBERT, MILTON,

DANTE AND ST JOHN

**METHUEN**
*London & New York*

First published in 1980 by
Methuen & Co. Ltd
11 New Fetter Lane, London EC4P 4EE
Published in the USA by Methuen & Co.
in association with Methuen, Inc.
733 Third Avenue, New York, NY 10017

© 1980 A. D. Nuttall

Phototypeset in V.I.P. Sabon by
Western Printing Services Ltd, Bristol
Printed in the United States of America

British Library Cataloguing in Publication Data

Nuttall, Anthony David
Overheard by God.
1. Herbert, George, b.1593. Temple, The
2. Milton, John. Paradise Lost
I. Title

821'.3    PP3507.T43

ISBN 0-416-73980-6

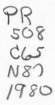

TO
DESMOND
HEATH

# CONTENTS

# PREFACE

The formal arrangement of this book may suggest that it was written with gradually declining energy: a fairly full treatment of Herbert's *The Temple* is followed by a much briefer account of Milton's *Paradise Lost*, which in turn is followed by essays on a single Canto by Dante and on the Gospel of St John. In fact the diminishing scale of the sections arises from a simple distaste for extended repetition. This study begins with an intuition: that for much of our older literature one may suppose the presence of an extra (inhuman) reader: that which is written for man is always and necessarily read also by God. The bourgeois marriage of poet and reader which now dominates literature and criticism was once infiltrated by a third party, whose claims are both more importunate and more absolute than those of any ordinary lover. This intuition is first tested on the poetry of Herbert, which was chosen for its power to bring out the greatest number of implications. Its subsequent application to Milton, Dante and St John is then relatively simple (though in each case – and especially the last – the argument is subjected to some fresh shock or challenge).

I have assumed without argument that love and charity lie at the heart of Christian morality, though the practice of particular Christians may on occasion have been very different. This assumption, I find, is welcomed by Christians and disputed by unbelievers. To me (an unbeliever) it seems merely obvious and I have therefore chosen not to support it with wearisome demonstration. Nevertheless, apart from this one intransigence,

I have profited greatly from the help and advice of friends and colleagues, especially Bernard Harrison, Michael Keefer, Laurence Lerner, Stephen Medcalf, Adrian Pinnington, Bernard Sharratt, Alan Sinfield, Michael Wadsworth and Sir Denys Wilkinson. I thank them all. My thanks are also due to Denise Pearson, for typing an almost illegible manuscript, to the Warden and Fellows of Merton College, Oxford, for allowing me the use of a guest-room when I needed to be near a great library, and to Desmond Heath, for lending me his flat when I needed silence.

Lewes, October 1979

# I. THE TEMPLE

## I

## THE PROBLEM

IMAGINE – if you can – God reading this poem:

### Dialogue

Sweetest Saviour, if my soul
  Were but worth the having,
Quickly should I then controll
  Any thought of waving.
But when all my care and pains
Cannot give the name of gains
To thy wretch so full of stains,
What delight or hope remains?

*What, Child, is the ballance thine,*
  *Thine the poise and measure?*
*If I say, Thou shalt be mine;*
  *Finger not my treasure.*
*What the gains in having thee*
*Do amount to, onely he,*
*Who for man was sold, can see;*
*That transferr'd th' accounts to me.*

But as I can see no merit,
    Leading to this favour:
So the way to fit me for it
    Is beyond my savour.
As the reason then is thine;
So the way is none of mine:
I disclaim the whole designe:
Sinne disclaims and I resigne.

*That is all, if that I could*
    *Get without repining;*
*And my clay, my creature, would*
    *Follow my resigning:*
*That as I did freely part*
*With my glorie and desert,*
*Left all joyes to feel all smart — —*
    Ah! no more: thou break'st my heart.[1]

Is God pleased with what he reads? The question put thus to a twentieth-century reader sounds almost idiotically bald, but few people of the seventeenth century would have regarded it as improper. There is of course a certain theological discomfort in the notion of *reading* (with its implication of consecutive apprehension) applied to one whose understanding is total and instantaneous, but this we can easily correct. As we do so, our phrase at once takes on a more seventeenth-century flavour: is this poem pleasing to God?

Our first answer is likely to be some sort of 'yes'. God cannot fail to be gratified to see his creature, George Herbert, so submissive to his will, so sensible of the sacrifice performed on his behalf. The Christian humility of the poem is perfect, except perhaps for one thing (and here we must press a little harder on our unimaginable image, God watching the growth of the poem from over Herbert's shoulder). The humility of the first stanza is of course deliberately presented by the poet as wrong-headed. Accordingly, it at once invites a loving correction from God. But before God can, so to speak, clear his

---

[1] This, and all subsequent quotations from Herbert, are taken from *The Works of George Herbert*, ed. F. E. Hutchinson, the 1967 corrected reprint of the first edition of 1941.

throat to answer, lo, the creature Herbert is scribbling away at the second stanza and God's part is there, written out neatly for him. Herbert in the poem does not simply submit himself to the will of God; he personally supplies the divine correction.

The first literary effect of this is to turn the 'George Herbert' who offers the first stanza into a dramatic character. The George Herbert who blushes and fidgets in the first stanza cannot be the same person as the George Herbert whose comprehensive (too comprehensive) piety produces the whole poem. Had the second stanza continued in the same mode and voice as the first, giving us in place of the divine response a change of attitude – say an expression of grateful acceptance – on *Herbert's* part, the split between author and speaker would never have become obvious. More importantly, the expression on the face of the divine eavesdropper might have remained benevolently unironic. As things are, a certain sense of incongruity is inescapable. Herbert, the character *within* the poem, displays the inept incomprehension of mere humanity, but Herbert the author undertakes to supply on God's behalf the answers only God can give.

The pattern in which Herbert's merely human conception of God is externally corrected recurs in his poetry. The voice ranting in his skull is silenced by another voice, half-heard, more distant and at the same time more intimate than the first, but fundamentally Other:

Methoughts I heard one calling Child.

Thus Herbert's poems dramatize one of the most important requirements of the religious temper, which is quite simply that God should be other than oneself. But by that very act of dramatizing (which is a kind of usurpation) they blaspheme it.

To suppose the immediate attention of God himself directed to all this fictive ingenuity is no wild assumption. On the contrary, it is a necessary implication of Christian doctrine. Moreover, as I have hinted, to imagine God so can prove instructive even for the modern, unbelieving student of literature. One immediate consequence of this rather odd exercise of the spiritual imagination is vastly to increase the difference between the poetry of Donne and the poetry of Herbert. The passing twinge of shame we feel on Herbert's behalf (akin to the social embarrassment we may feel on behalf of a precociously intelligent child) rarely if ever visits the reader of Donne. Donne the suppliant and Donne the poet remain one, truly humble flesh.

The logical knot of Herbert's poetry can be drawn still tighter, until presumption becomes something like sheer contradiction. Herbert, a mere man, explains on God's behalf the things which man is incapable of seeing for himself; but since it is a man who does this explaining, it cannot after all be true that man is thus incapable. Philosophers will easily recognize the salient features of this battle-scarred terrain. They may think of Sartre, who sought to explain in words the inefficacy of language, or of the logical positivists, who offered the proposition (itself neither analytical nor based on sense-perception) that all meaningful propositions are either analytic or based on sense-perception. But is the devotional poetry of Herbert really self-destructive in this way? There seems to be a case (at the very least) for saying, 'No, it is not'.

The best and most nearly complete answer is that which refers us to Revelation and tradition. Herbert, in putting words into the mouth of God, is not attempting some grotesque act of up-staging; he is merely doing what Christians, as part of a dynamic religious tradition, have always done, that is, rephrase and re-point the eternal truths of the faith. The faith of Islam confines its adherents to the petrified text of the Koran. This has never been the Christian way. What else does the parish priest do each Sunday but speak on behalf of God in his interpretation of Scripture? Seen in this light, Herbert's poetic practices may no longer appear as an idiosyncratic aberration but rather a natural extension of his ordinary duties as Rector of Bemerton.

Does this, then, abolish our difficulty? It is likely that most practising priests would answer that it does not. Even in the pulpit the special embarrassment of the modest man entrusted with a most immodest task is common, for all that the speaker is physically exalted and sustained above the heads of his congregation, is softly fenced in with the symbols of his traditional office. In the terms of current criticism, the church, the vestments, the pulpit provide a supportive semasiological apparatus, one function of which is to impersonalize the speaker's words. Yet even so the better sort of priest will tell you that he can hardly recall his own sermons without a kind of shame. It is therefore hardly surprising that in the personal mode of a devotional lyric (in which an immediate intercourse between God and the subject is proposed) this feeling of shame is instantly exacerbated. Herbert, quite clearly, felt it. Moreover, in the case of the devotional poetry there are strong theological grounds for this disquiet. To be sure, the Protestant answer to the parson's modest doubts has always been that they are or should be merely irrelevant. It is not the man who speaks but God who speaks in him, and behind this lies the austere Augustinian doctrine that all the good we do is really done by God working in us. But notice that this answer is more applicable to the pronouncements of the priest to his flock than it is to that strange activity called prayer, in which the subject habitually finds himself drawn to *supply* harsh answers from his unseen, inaudible interlocutor.

Let us consider an artificial example:

Lord, give me a thousand pounds. Ah, Lord, but now I see that to ask for a thousand pounds may be mere greed. Be it then according to thy will.

Notice that in this fairly typical prayer, there are, so to speak, two selves. There is the baser self, which asks, and there is the higher self, which cancels the request. The relation of the baser self to God is unreflective. The higher self, on the other hand, rationalizes its relation to God. It is consciously theological. The consequence of this increased consciousness is an immediate loss of that innocence in which alone petitionary prayer is morally possible. Once the thought has occurred that God both knows what ought to be done and will in any case do what ought to be done, one is hard put to it to avoid a second thought: petitionary prayer is otiose. The fact that God might have responded to an innocent petition, artlessly offered, is now irrelevant. Indeed, it could be said that the language of the phrase 'petitionary prayer is otiose' is redundant: prayer *is* petition, *is* a kind of asking. Prayer itself, therefore, becomes otiose, and is replaced by a lordly gesture of assent. And if human petition is otiose, human approval of God's freedom of action, or human permission to God to exercise his will is still more plainly otiose. It might be supposed that the pattern of thought in this particular specimen of self-cancelling prayer is so clear that a few repetitions would convince the subject that it might be discontinued forthwith. Yet it appears that many Christians persevere with it throughout their lives, embarking each night upon a petition which they must know will be withdrawn before the sentence is completed. Many of Herbert's poems are in this sense not prayers so much as modest refusals to pray. The better self in my specimen ended by saying, 'Be it then according to thy will'. Clearly, this with no great violence could be re-expressed as 'But thou wilt say to me, "These things are not for men to describe".' Now we have a formal example of speaking on behalf of God, or ascribing words to God. Protestantism has two ways of construing this better self. One is to call it 'conscience', the other is to invoke the notion of grace.

It seems plain that the first of these, 'conscience' will be of small service to us in our present difficulty. If we say that conscience may properly supply the presumable answers of God we give our assent to what must now be seen as a venial fiction. God has not in fact spoken by a direct and miraculous intervention; rather, conscience has supplied the better thought. It soon becomes apparent that this scheme is not adequate to contain the spiritual drama of Herbert's poetry. Herbert repeatedly shows us in his poems how the merely human is broken in upon by something which is not human, is not natural at all, is God himself. Take these lines (from *Love III*):

> Love bade me welcome: yet my soul drew back,
>     Guiltie of dust and sinne.
> But quick-ey'd Love, observing me grow slack
>     From my first entrance in,
> Drew nearer to me, sweetly questioning,
>     If I lack'd any thing.

A guest, I answer'd, worthy to be here:
Love said, You shall be he.
I the unkinde, ungratefull? Ah my deare,
I cannot look on thee.
Love took my hand, and smiling did reply
Who made the eyes but I?

If (forgetting style and metre for a moment) we substitute
'Conscience reminds us that God would say' for 'love said' in
the second stanza, the effect of a subjective universe shattered
from without is virtually lost.

If anyone here answers, 'But the voice of conscience is *sim-pliciter* the voice of God', I might begin by querying that
*simpliciter*. Certainly in *Love III* we cannot substitute 'consci-ence' for 'Love' without some very odd results:

Conscience took my hand, and smiling did reply
Who made the eyes but I?

But of course the basic suggestion that to the Protestant mind
God is present in the movements of conscience is perfectly
sound. If we stress this aspect of conscience we shall find that
we have really already moved to the second major explanation
of 'the better self', namely *grace*.

The doctrine of grace at once confronts us with an almost
frighteningly complete solution of our problem. For to say that
grace produces the utterances of the better self is to say that
these utterances are not in fact the work of a *self* at all, but the
work of God. And this in blunt terms means that while George
Herbert may be said to have written the first and third stanzas
of *Dialogue*, God actually wrote the second and fourth stanzas.
Thus the poem is not a dramatization of the relation between
God and man but is an actual example of it. It is not a mimetic
performance but is a recorded conversation which once took
place between Herbert and God. One is tempted to add that the
very authorship of *The Temple* now becomes a dual affair.
Herbert wrote most of it, but God wrote quite a lot. Moreover,
we now lose our distinction between Herbert the dramatic
character who frets in the first stanza and Herbert the poet
whose comprehensive theological understanding supplies the

rest. Herbert the man collapses back into Herbert the character. Such is the radical interpretation.

A more moderate application of Protestant theology might allow to Herbert the poet, as distinct from Herbert the dramatic character, the role of versifying the communications of grace and of incorporating them into an artistic whole. This, it will be noticed, has an immediate ring of sanity. The 'joint-authorship' account is simply incredible, and this is no less true, I fancy, for the seventeenth-century mind than it is for the twentieth-century mind. But that Herbert might have believed himself to be modifying and re-phrasing impulses vouchsafed to him by God seems entirely possible.

The only trouble with the moderate account is that it read-mits the demon we have been labouring to expel. For, clearly, the George Herbert who wrote the whole poem has his own moral and artistic purposes in phrasing God's communication as he does. The 'better self' is with us once more and is in a manner 'using' the good insights granted by God. This 'using' is partly aesthetic. God's communications are given a high finish and a certain metrical form in order that they may harmonize with the rest. The distinction I assume here between a supposedly simple Godly insight and the 'worked up' poetic version may seem a little forced. A reading of the *Jordan* poems, however, should soon convince the reader that the distinction was perfectly real to Herbert.

> *What, Child, is the ballance thine*
> *Thine the poise and measure?*
> *If I say, Thou shalt be mine;*
> *Finger not my treasure.*
> *What the gains in having thee*
> *Do amount to, onely he,*
> *Who for man was sold, can see;*
> *That transferr'd th' accounts to me.*

These words are God's but at the same time they are very evidently Herbert's. If we read as historians of ideas we may well miss the crucial point here. To the alert literary critic it is surely inescapable. The elegantly chiastic repetition of 'thine', the hushed meiosis of 'transferr'd th' accounts to me' are especially Herbertian. Thus these divine yet Herbertian stanzas work in the moral economy of the poem (in the teeth of all Calvinist disclaimers of human merit) to establish a kind of moral credit for Herbert. How else, after all, did he earn his reputation for sanctity and virtue? By a paradox familiar to readers of Protestant literature the disclaiming of merit is somehow felt to be itself meritorious. There is a sense that Herbert has, after all, got in first with the right sentiment.

Yet none of this will quite do. Again we need to imagine God ruefully smiling to find his words anticipated. Or perhaps not smiling. It is hard to believe that Herbert did not foresee that these stanzas would enhance his reputation for piety. The insinuation of sanctity by disclaiming sanctity is horribly close (in an intelligent poet) to bad faith. And Herbert was very intelligent.

---

## II

---

## THE ESCAPE THROUGH FICTION

I HAVE argued that a sense of impropriety, of some degree of personal usurpation in Herbert's divine speeches persists, after the various theological excuses have been exhausted. This thesis, however, is open to an objection of quite a different kind. All our difficulties, it might be said, spring from an elementary confusion. What we have been treating as prayers in poetic form are really poems which imitate or represent prayer. They are from first to last dramatic fictions, with (as commonly) a fictional addressee within the poem – God – and a real addressee outside the poem – the reader. The thought of God eavesdropping on their composition holds no terrors, since he will most certainly understand them for what they are, pictures of the way a man might pray.

Now in the world of fiction it is commonly assumed that the mode of expression need not be realistically compatible with that which is expressed. For example, a Shakespearean character may affirm in excellent blank verse that he has no ear for poetry. To conclude that he is a liar or a fool, to tax him with his perfect cadences, is *logically* absurd. The 'I' of much love poetry is obviously fictional in a similar way. The lover in the poem may cry out that he is in every way exhausted, while the author may betray in the vigour of his writing a state of abounding imaginative health. The conventions of fiction easily permit all this. So with the poetry of Herbert: there need be nothing disingenuous or contradictory in the fact that the George Herbert who prays *within* the poem misconstrues his faith while George Herbert the author stage-manages the misconstruction, since the Herbert who exists within the poem is himself merely a fictional construct. The language given to God likewise exists on a plane of pure fiction. Remember the words of Aristotle: history tells us 'what Alcibiades did' but tragedy tells us 'what would happen' (*Poetics*, 1451b). Herbert's poetry does not pretend to give us what God said, it gives us through the well-known and accepted conventions of fiction what God *would* say. As soon as we see this, it could be said, the supposed offence of Herbert in answering for God is much reduced. To say what God would say, to explore the hypothetical, is after all very close to the professional duty of the priest discussed earlier. Thus, it may be thought, the heat is off. Herbert is not shouldering God aside in the very act of prayer, correcting his own human inadequacy with a blasphemous anticipation of the divine response; he is rather projecting upon the screen of English literature a representation in profile of the ways in which God's love meets, frustrates and exalts the praying human subject.

Now even if this account were true we must once again insist that while it may indeed reduce the urgency of our problem it certainly does not remove it altogether. Even if Herbert were giving us not prayers, but pictures of prayers, some mimetic fidelity to the real conditions of prayer must presumably be required. It would be an insult to the faithful to offer them a representation of prayer which confessed no obligation to notice what prayer is actually like. There is indeed a sense in which our original hesitation over the propriety of providing answers for God is actually underlined when fictional status is assigned to them. Within the poem we are told that the one element which can save the praying subject from a hopeless subjectivism is the voice from outside. But now we are assured that the words of God are a fiction. The one element which could mitigate our human isolation and disclose the divine substance (the one element which, incidentally, is absent from ordinary prayer) is feigned by the poet.

There is a curious analogy here with the novels of Virginia Woolf. There, because of the chosen mode of writing, the reader is confined to a single stream of subjective consciousness. Moreover, there seems to be implicit in this choice of mode a certain philosophical claim, that really the world is like this. Not surprisingly, the reader soon finds himself a prey to solipsistic unease. But this unease is magically dispelled by Virginia Woolf's employment of a plurality of consciousnesses. As we step from the mind of Lily Briscoe into the mind of Mrs Ramsay, the world of the novel reassumes its proper solidity. A thing which can be seen from more than one side must be three-dimensional; the perceptions of Paul can after all be corrected externally – by the perceptions of Charles. And so, we may suppose, all is well again. But this power of passing from mind to mind, which alone can confer reality on things, is possible only in fiction. This generates the absurd conclusion that fiction can give us real substance while reality cannot.

Of course there are some writers who emphasize the spurious licence of fiction to heal and cure in order to make a sardonic point about the real sickness of things. Such, in the view of some critics, was Fielding's purpose when, by an ostentatiously improbable exertion of comic vicissitude, he repeatedly saved Tom Jones from the likely consequences of his thoughtlessness. He was thus a better moralist than Sir John Hawkins or Dr Johnson took him for, since, so far from exalting natural impulse and letting the rest go hang, his very comic extravagance, rightly understood, implies strong support for an ethic of considerate and responsible action: those who rely so heavily upon the saving intervention of the comic spirit *ex machina* are surely not to be themselves relied upon in ordinary life, where the Comic Spirit has no power to save. That Fielding may have worked to this end is perhaps just credible. But that Herbert should have sought by the incongruously obtrusive availability of God in his poems to apPraise his readers of the real unavailability of God is simply incredible.

The argument I have stated can be blurred in various ways. That the voice of God, coming from outside the natural order, can alone illumine the benighted condition of merely natural man – all this is perfectly fair as an account of the state of affairs proposed in the poetry of Herbert. But the notion of God's external voice is really ambiguous. In my argument it was suggested that the one sufficient remedy was an actual, audible reply. Thus the *fact* of a reply, it was implied, is in a way more crucial than the *content* of the reply. But this audible reply (it was pointed out) is precisely what does *not* occur in real prayer (outside the special experiences of mystics). This antithesis between fact and content is, however, misleading. The very nature of Christ's teaching proclaims it Other than the world, and this *fact about content* supplies an adequate external corrective to the merely human. This would mean that the fiction whereby Herbert has God speak at the end of the poem becomes after all a venial fiction, since it is no longer on the *fact* of a *heard* reply that the very existence of an external correction depends.

Yet it is somehow exceedingly difficult to get rid utterly of the sense that Herbert has – for whatever excellent purpose – 'taken over' the speech of God. Take *The Quip*:

> The merrie world did on a day
> With his train-bands and mates agree
> To meet together, where I lay,
> And all in sport to geere at me.
>
> First, Beautie crept into a rose,
> Which when I pluckt not, Sir, said she,
> Tell me, I pray, Whose hands are those?
> *But thou shalt answer, Lord, for me.*
>
> Then Money came, and chinking still,
> What tune is this, poore man? said he:
> I heard in Musick you had skill.
> *But thou shalt answer, Lord, for me.*

Then came brave Glorie puffing by
In silks that whistled, who but he?
He scarce allow'd me half an eie.
*But thou shalt answer, Lord, for me.*

Then came quick Wit and Conversation,
And he would needs a comfort be,
And, to be short, make an Oration.
*But thou shalt answer, Lord, for me.*

Yet when the houre of thy designe
To answer these fine things shall come;
Speak not at large; say, I am thine:
And then they have their answer home.

Here if ever Herbert is in fine form. The swift allegorical
sketches — sly Beauty, creeping into her rose, provoking
Money, jangling his coins, Glory in his 'whistling' silks and
that darting allusion to the 'and to be brief, Gentlemen' em-
ployed by all really prolix speakers — these have something of
the vigour of the droll mediaeval figures in the *Ancrene Wisse*
together with the added grace and wit of one who has moved —
and enjoyed moving — in courtly circles. Herbert the artist is in
high good humour. But what does the poem say? It says that it
would be wrong for Herbert to give God's answer and then,
instead of lapsing into a devout silence, actually *tells* God what
to say! To be sure, the phrase God is asked to pronounce
proclaims his ownership of Herbert, but, if that is so, why
cannot he be allowed to say so for himself — especially as the
poem has told the reader four times that that is what must
happen? The whole poem takes its tone from the bad company
it ostensibly rejects. It is *bumptious*. Herbert loves to present
himself as the helpless child of God. Here the child, cuckoo-
like, has somehow outgrown his nourisher and seems to nudge
his exhausted protector into the required behaviour.

Note that with this poem we cannot say that Herbert the
character defers to God, while Herbert the author supplies the
conventional divine reply. Within the fiction of the poem it is
the same George Herbert which defers to and instructs his
creator.

Thus, even if we take the poems as radical fictions, difficulties persist. But in truth they are not fictions. We are not dealing with an Ovidian or a Cavalier, but with the author of the *Jordan* poems. Herbert was a strict Protestant and he did not hold with playing games. Indeed the *Jordan* poems are the final test of the 'games' view of Herbert.

### Jordan I

Who sayes that fictions onely and false hair
Become a verse? Is there in truth no beautie?
Is all good structure in a winding stair?
May no lines passe, except they do their dutie
    Not to a true, but painted chair?

Is it no verse, except enchanted groves
And sudden arbours shadow course-spunne lines?
Must purling streams refresh a lovers loves?
Must all be vail'd, while he that reades, divines,
    Catching the sense at two removes?

Shepherds are honest people; let them sing:
Riddle who list, for me, and pull for Prime:
I envie no mans nightingale or spring;
Nor let them punish me with losse of rime,
    Who plainly say, *My God, My King.*

### Jordan II

When first my lines of heav'nly joyes made mention,
Such was their lustre, they did so excell,
That I sought out quaint words, and trim invention;
My thoughts began to burnish, sprout, and swell,
Curling with metaphors a plain intention,
Decking the sense, as if it were to sell.

Thousands of notions in my brain did runne,
Off'ring their service, if I were not sped:
I often blotted what I had begunne;
This was not quick enough, and that was dead.
Nothing could seem too rich to clothe the sunne,
Much lesse those joyes which trample on his head.

As flames do work and winde, when they ascend,
So did I weave my self into the sense.
But while I bustled, I might heare a friend
Whisper, *How wide is all this long pretence!*
*There is in love a sweetnesse readie penn'd:*
*Copie out onely that, and save expense.*

Modern readers of Herbert, faced with these poems, show
an extraordinary tendency to flee to inessentials. Thus it is
customary to draw laborious distinctions between them: in
*Jordan I* Herbert is happy to let the rest write pretty poems and
merely expresses a personal preference for another mode, but
in *Jordan II* he is simply telling the story of his own develop-
ment from an ornate to a plain style – and so forth. It is surely
better to face the matter squarely. The *Jordan* poems have the
same title because they are at bottom the same poem. In these
poems Herbert is not saying that some sorts of poetry are nicer
than others; he is saying that poetry itself must at last be burned
away by truth. Why are the poems called *Jordan*? Because the
poet is crossing the river beyond which nothing less than the
most perfect simplicity is tolerated. As Stanley Fish has admir-
ably insisted,[2] Herbert learns in the *Jordan* poems that there is
nothing for *him* to write at all: a 'plain style' is not the solution,
but is rather, 'the last infirmity of the noble poetic mind'.

And, of course, this mid-river poetry is crucified by inconsis-
tency. It is, necessarily, poetically parasitic upon the devices it
so austerely renounces. I say 'necessarily' because that which is
renounced is finally poetry, *simpliciter*. The poem tells us that
all we need to say is 'My God, My King', but *that* is not a poem,
and Herbert the artist must needs leave us more (even while
telling us that in God's eye this 'more' is really 'less'). To read
the *Jordan* poems in succession is to experience the contradic-
tion all the more poignantly. For even the pretext of a valedic-
tion, a last venial farewell to poetry, can scarcely be sustained
when the exercise is *repeated*. To misquote Heraclitus, no man
passes twice over the same Jordan. Herbert cannot let go.

But in any case the inconsistency is inescapable within the

---

[2] *Self-consuming Artifacts: The Experience of Seventeenth-Century Litera-
ture*, Berkeley, Los Angeles and London, 1973, pp. 198–9.

confines of a single *Jordan* poem. If Herbert really means it when he says that 'My God, My King' is enough, why did he not cancel all that went before? The answer is not, 'Well then, he does not really mean it.' He does mean it and he is riven. We insult him if we pretend otherwise.

Nevertheless my imagined opponent may still fight back. That Herbert should in a poem explicitly renounce poetry will scarcely surprise the educated reader. The renunciation of art in favour of nature is after all one of the older tropes of the conscious artist. Style is an infinitely elastic medium. It expands to embrace the very rejection of style until that rejection is at last — a style. In *Jordan II* 'as if it were to sell' may be read by one reader as an idiosyncratic flicker of Puritan contempt, but another, more knowing reader will see in it a *literary* echo — 'I will not praise that purpose not to sell'. Further examples are easily found: *Ingenium nobis ipsa puella facit*; 'Foole, said my Muse to me, looke in thy heart and write'; 'Sans sans, I pray you'.[3] The game is an old one; why should not Herbert be playing like the rest?

There is perhaps a sense in which Herbert may be drawn by what may be termed the purely literary impulse of his writing into this game. But at the same time he resists with a resistance which is partly extra-literary. For, after all, Herbert really was a Protestant parson. Certain radical elements in Protestant thought really did imply the rejection of poetry. Even in the eighteenth century Dr Johnson could still feel that religious poetry was infected with a kind of duplicity,[4] and of course this duplicity approaches most nearly to mendacity in those poets who profess a severely Protestant approach. T. S. Eliot once observed that complete atheists are incapable of genuine blasphemy.[5] *Credo quia absurdum*. It is *because* Herbert lies and blasphemes that we know he is a great religious poet. The player-poet, on the other hand, is safe, for he 'nothing affirmeth'.

In saying this I deliberately break a circle which we have all

---

[3] *Seriatim*, Shakespeare, Sonnet XXI; Propertius, *Elegies*, II. i.4; Sidney, *Astrophil and Stella*, 1; Shakespeare, *Loves Labour's Lost*, v. ii. 416.

[4] 'Life of Waller', in his *Lives of the Poets*, ed. G. B. Hill, 1905, vol. I, p. 291.

[5] 'Baudelaire', in *Selected Essays*, 1951, p. 421.

been taught, first by the New Critics and after them by the structuralists, to regard as sacred. This is the principle by which any work of art is permitted to propose its own inviolable limits of reference. In real life opinions catch and rub on one another; continuities are demanded and inconsistencies condemned. But, if, say, *Sailing to Byzantium* commends the inhuman and *The Circus Animals' Desertion* commends the human, it is gauche (we are told) to speak of a conflict, or even a change of mind. They are merely different poems. Attempts have been made, indeed, to extend the principle further. After Wittgenstein many philosophers proposed that what had previously been thought of as inconsistencies should be not so much solved as dissolved, conjured away. We were to do this by referring the seemingly discordant elements to separate, encapsulated 'language games'. This book is written in a contrary spirit. Instead, it proposes a world of warm connection and violent collision and a literature everywhere rent and energized by commerce with that world.

The polite assumption that all systems are separate and closed has had its effect not only on literary criticism but also on the history of ideas. Philosophical or ideological theories are treated as cultural phenomena rather than as propositions which may be true or false. The effect is to emasculate critical enquiry. For example, it is somehow bad form to describe a given body of thought in any other terms than would be accepted by the original proponent. To say 'Calvinism is antinomianism' is to be met with the pained rejoinder, 'No, no, antinomian is a term of abuse; you cannot have read Calvin'. The possibility that Calvin may have flinched from or failed to perceive the real implications of his thought is set aside as illogical; the thought and his version of the thought are one and the same. Reasoning is thus flattened, made two-dimensional. The third dimension, the dimension of implication and consequence, the proper arena of criticism, at once apparent to any one who reads his Calvin with the question 'Is this true?' in his mind – this is utterly abolished. In what follows I propose to ignore this taboo and to reassert our ancient liberties.

Certainly the old poets never thought themselves confined to a uniformly fictitious realm. They themselves break the sacred circle again and again. Herbert does so, quite clearly, in *The Dedication* (itself a poem) prefixed to *The Temple*:

## The Dedication

*Lord, my first fruits present themselves to thee;*
*Yet not mine neither: for from thee they came,*
*And must return. Accept of them and me,*
*And make us strive, who shall sing best thy name.*
*Turn their eyes hither, who shall make a gain:*
*Theirs, who shall hurt themselves or me, refrain.*

The fatal interaction of real and fictional universes is here implicit in the very form. Dedications are necessarily done not by the characters within poems but by authors. Thus, at the very beginning of *The Temple* the relation between Herbert the poet and Herbert the worshipper is insistently problematic. The poems are themselves offered to God. This at once confounds our neat resolution of difficulties whereby God was allowed to be the addressee within the poem while outside it was the reader who was addressed. A dedication, merely by being a dedication, refers to the poems as poems and therefore stands outside their fictional preserve. Yet even in the dedication Herbert addresses God, and does so in verse which is very like what follows in the main body of the text. Of course, he knows that *The Temple* consists of poems which will be read by people, and in a sense the poems are written for these people – or at least for those of them who may obtain spiritual profit. Again one is reminded of the village priest, who prays to God indeed, but with one eye, so to speak, on his congregation. He must adjust his language to their needs and all his persuasion of God must at the same time persuade his human listeners. In such a situation, one might say, rhetoric which cannot properly be directed at God has nevertheless an acceptable function. The rhetoric is for the congregation. But in fact it is rarely possible for a man placed in such a situation to remain so artificially clear-headed. And, even if he did, the spectacle might not be entirely pleasing. If we insist that the dedication is just a poem like the rest and so preserve the fictional closure, the sentiments expressed in it become an ingenious, illusionist joke, an amusing reference to a state of affairs which would exist if real prayer were going on. But Herbert's dedication is not a joke, and has never been taken so by generations of qualified readers, that is, by poetry-loving Christians.

In fact the 'games' view of Herbert is under attack from two sides at once. It is fought, with deadly seriousness, in the poems and it is virtually outlawed, or at least threatened, by the Protestant theology which Herbert the man accepted. I do not argue either that Protestantism or Herbert was consistently and at all times committed to the extreme Puritan rejection of fiction. But I do argue that the extreme Puritan position was, at the very least, felt by him to be relevant and formidable. The one reply he would never have made is, 'Oh, but that wasn't me speaking; it was a fictional *persona*; it is only a poem, you see.' Even if we suppose that Herbert's Protestantism may have allowed him the occasional trope or metaphor, there is one trope which he could never use with an easy consciousness of fiction, and that is the trope of pretended simplicity. That Herbert should have offered as a sophisticated joke something which corresponds in every particular with a treasured belief is, once more, simply incredible. The situation has its ironies. The New Critics and the structuralists are ideologically committed to preserving the separate autonomy of fiction; Herbert as poet falls naturally within this field. But Herbert also, three centuries and more before the first of the New Critics reared his head, belongs to a faction which is identifiably opposed to theirs. Thus in engaging with Herbert they are dealing with a poet whose very concept of composition is on their terms impermissible. F. R. Leavis, on the other hand, falls (by this broadest of classifications) on Herbert's side. Incorrigibly Leavis connected literature with reality and had the scars to prove it. The word (it is not quite un-usable) which links Herbert and Leavis is of course 'Puritan'.

The hard thing having been said, it is now necessary to say the softer things. Herbert's attitude to fiction is not always so unkind. He can offer God 'a *wreathed* garland of deserved praise' (*A Wreath*) and in *A True Hymne* he affirms that the simple words, 'My joy, my life, my Crown' are 'among the best *in art*', so reconciling art and truth. In the second Latin poem addressed to his mother Herbert praises both her piety and her style (*scriptio*) and grants that while the greatest beauty lay in the kernel, some was to be found in the shell:

*Bellum putamen, nucleus bellissimus*

Again, it is well known and may indeed be relevant that Anglicans of Herbert's stamp allowed the propriety of beautiful church furnishing (the Lutheran Church, says Herbert, is 'shie of dressing'[6]). Herbert's friend, Nicholas Ferrar, in *The Winding Sheet* frankly grants that flourishes of style are 'gracefull when they fall in naturally of themselves'[7] and certainly makes free use of them in his own writing. But such Anglican softening to external beauty is constantly thwarted and opposed by a fiercer asceticism. 'Roses and lilies speak of God', says Herbert, significantly enough in one of the two sonnets addressed to his mother, but in *The Quip* the rose is seen as something sinister, an emblem of seduction, and in the poem which is actually called *The Rose* this theme recurs. The reflex of feeling is typical. 'My joy, my life, my Crown' may be called for a moment 'among the best in art' but we all know that these words alone do not compose a poem and are in this regard exactly parallel to 'My God, My King' in *Jordan I*. Nicholas Ferrar, immediately after the words we quoted a moment ago, adds that really a plain style is best and before he died made a great bonfire of all his books of literature, 'many Hundreths in all kind of Languages, which he had in all places gotten with great search, and some cost. . . . Comedies, Tragedies, Love-Hymns, Heroicall Poems, and such like.' So great was the smoke that men came running from the fields, 'and within a few dayes, it was by rumour spread at Market Townes all the country over, that Mr. Nic: Ferrar lay a dying, but could not dye till he had burned all his Conjuring-Bookes. . . .' As he lay, waiting for death, he wrote, 'The having an Orlando in the house, is sufficient ground to have it burnt down over their heads, that truly feare God'.[8] The hold of Augustine and of

[6] *The British Church*, in *Works*, p. 110.
[7] *The Ferrar Papers*, ed. B. Blackstone, 1938, p. 200. See also Patrick Grant, *The Transformation of Sin*, Montreal, London and Amherst, 1974, p. 34.
[8] John Ferrar, 'A Life of Nicholas Ferrar', in *The Ferrar Papers*, pp. 60, 61, 63.

Calvin had hardly begun to weaken. *Quid Athenae Hierosolymis?*

---

## III

---

## CALVIN'S GHOST

THE *Short Title Catalogue* (1475–1640) lists no fewer than 96 editions of Calvin's writings and 50 of Beza. These easily head the list (Luther and Bullinger come next with 38 each). Each of the years between 1548 and 1634 saw the publication of one work or more by Calvin. Between 1578 and 1581 there were six to eight every year. Calvin's record of publications in English was not overtaken until the early seventeeth century, and then it was by William Perkins and Henry Smith, both Calvinists. The influence of Calvin on the Thirty-nine Articles is crushingly evident. Article ix affirms that all men naturally deserve damnation and adds that this infection of nature persists even in the regenerate. Article x asserts the spiritual and moral impotence of man: 'We have no power to good works . . . without the grace of God' and Article xi adds that we are accounted righteous before God only by the merit of Christ. Article xii explains that good works, so called, can in no way endure the severity of God's judgement and are pleasing to him only because they are a sign of faith. Works done *before* grace, meanwhile, are 'not pleasing to God and have the nature of Sin' (Article xiii). This doctrine was anathematized by the Council of Trent at its sixth session, in January 1547.[9] The germ of Calvinism lies, as W. H. Halewood observes,[10] not so much in Augustine as in Paul's Epistle to the Galatians. Christ is the only possible agent of salvation; to hope for salvation under

---

[9] See H. Denzinger (ed)., *Enchiridion Symbolorum, Definitionum et Declarationum de Rebus Fidei et Morum*, revised A. Schönmatzer, 23 edn, Rome, 1965, p. 378.
[10] *The Poetry of Grace: Reformation Themes and Structures in English Seventeenth Century Poetry*, New Haven and London, 1970, p. 36.

the law is to put faith in the saving power of human effort, which in Paul's view is a ridiculous blasphemy. The contrast is thus made absolute between, on the one hand, God, spirit, faith and salvation and, on the other, Man, flesh, law and damnation.

But there Augustine enters. The doctrine of *Galatians* might almost have been deduced independently from Augustine's Platonizing insistence that God is not just good; he is good-*ness*.[11] Whenever our actions are good, they have goodness in them, and where there is goodness, there is God, and where there is God, there are not we. It is characteristic of the Reformation not to soften the edges of these doctrines but rather to harden them. The Thirty-nine Articles tell us that 'good works' before grace are not pleasing to God, but Luther goes further. He suggests that a sinful nature might be a positive recommendation in the eyes of God: 'If I am unfit for prayer because of my sins, well and good. I do not want to become more fit. For, alas, to God I am more than fit for prayer because I am an exceedingly great sinner.'[12] Sin alone permits the triumphant operation of grace. Luther asks, 'What connection could there be between abundant mercy and human holiness?'[13] In his commentary on *Galatians* he reaffirms[14] that 'Christ was given, not . . . for small sins, but for great and huge sins' and adds a moment later that really monstrous sins, so far from placing us in the Devil's power, are really our best armour against him. Well might Satan feel confused. Luther joyously concludes with the words which were to fire the controversy between Major and Amsdorf, 'My righteousness does me no good but rather puts me at a disadvantage before God.'[15] Such language must strike us as seriously unbalanced. Yet when we encounter similar sentiments in Augustine it is fairly easy to see a kind of splendour in them, partly because we sense that Augustine is grappling with the appalling complacency of late

[11] *Confessions*, VII. iii. 5.
[12] Commentary on Psalm 51, in *Luther's Works*, ed. Jaroslav Pelikan, vol. XII, St Louis, 1955, p. 319.
[13] ibid., p. 324.
[14] *Works*, vol. XXVI, 1963, p. 35.
[15] ibid., p. 36.

Roman stoicism, 'the rational man armed in his virtue' and the like, and partly because Augustine's thought it always more dialectical, less brutally simple than Luther's. Yet Luther was no crank, but a revered and highly effective figure.

Nevertheless, the special violence of Luther's intelligence can never have been general. There can be no doubt that the ordinary religion of Protestant England was never so paradoxical as this. But Luther's extravagance is always rational, which is as much as to say that the inferences he makes *might* at any point be made by others, for they follow of themselves. His most extreme conclusions really are latent in the common theology. As a guide to ordinary assumptions he is indeed uncertain; as a guide to the occasional, half-suppressed terrors of the intelligent he may be very good indeed.

Calvin, whose style is altogether quieter, is more radical still. God the Father, he explains, really hates us:

> Because oure minde can neither desirously enoughe take holde of life in the mercie of God, nor receive it with suche thankfulnesse as we ought, but when it is before striken and throwne downe wyth the feare of the wrath of God and drede of eternal death, we are so taught by holy Scripture, that *wythout Christe wee maye see God in manner wrath-fully bent againste us, and his hande armed to our destruction:* that wee maye embrace hys goodwyll and fatherly kindnesse no otherwere, but in Christe.[16]

The italics are mine. It would appear that we have only one friend in the Trinity. The Father is our enemy. Blake's Urizen is no harsh caricature of Calvin's God-the-Father, but is if anything a more sympathetic figure than the original.

Thus Calvin begins to build for us the character of God, compounded, it would seem, of a hostile (and omnipotent) Father, a loving (and omnipotent) Son and an (omnipotent) Spirit. So far, so disquieting. As we read on, the picture, so far from lightening, grows darker. Calvin proceeds to clarify this obscure, troubling personality, not by explaining away the

[16] *The Institution of Christian Religion ... Translated into English* (by Thomas Norton), 1561, II. xvi. 2, fol. 95 *verso*, hereafter referred to as 'Institutes'.

hatred (which he considers manifestly just) but by weakening the love:

> For God whyche is the hyghest ryghteousnesse, can not love wickednesse whiche he seeth in us all. Therfore we al have in us that, which is worthy of the hatred of God.[17]

And at once he explains that God's only motive for loving us at all, in the person of Christ, is that he 'wyll not lose that which ys his in us'.

One's first response to the proposition that the Father hates us while the Son loves is to conclude that the Father is no Christian. For him, justice is not transcended by love; for that mystery we must turn to the Son. Bizarre as the notion must appear, there is a certain symmetry in the idea that of the persons of the Trinity it is Christ who is the Christian. But this makeshift comfort proves short-lived. Christ, after all, loves us only as one loves his property; he trembles for us only as one trembles for an endangered investment. The grim doctrine of Article ix is easily recognized: 'We are all . . . borne to damnation of hell.'[18] All that is good is God's; the rest is uniformly black, with no gradations. It might be objected that to argue thus is to imply that there is no moral difference between man and Satan. Calvin does not shrink from this conclusion, but eagerly embraces it. He quotes[19] with pure approval the following words from Augustine's commentary on the Gospel of John (XLIL.xl.8):

> Let no man flatter himself; *of himself he is Satan.* His blessing comes from God alone. For what do you have of your own but sin?[20]

I have given the passage in the modern translation of Ford Lewis Battles. The sixteenth-century translator, Thomas Norton, may have found it hard to stomach, for he flinches from

---

[17] ibid., II. xvi. 3, fol. 95 *verso*.
[18] ibid., LL. xvi. 3, fol. 95 *verso*.
[19] *Institutes of the Christian Religion*, ed. J. T. McNeill, trans. Ford Lewis Battles, Library of Christian Classics, II. ii. 11, vol. 1, p. 269; in Norton's translation, fol. 10 *recto*.
[20] In J.-P. Migne, *Patrologiae Cursus Completus (Patrologia Latina)* vol. xxv, Paris, 1845, p. 1750.

the frontal specificity of 'Satan' and writes instead 'hee is a devill'. The doctrine is indeed stark. In so far as man exists separately from God, he sins. *Esse est peccare.* 'Of oure selves wee are nothing but evell.'[21]

It may be thought that in one respect we must have overstated the case: that, while every *moral* act of man is thus tainted, there exists a considerable territory – the operations, say, of pure reason – which may be thought of as morally neutral. Here perhaps is space to lick our wounds? Not so. Calvin will have none of this. His thought is fiercely binary and tends always to the elimination of middle terms. *Everything* we do is wicked; certainly our reasoning is thus:

> Therefore mans reason neither approcheth, nor goeth towarde, nor ones directeth syghte unto this trueth. . . .
> But bicause we being dronke with a false persuasion of oure owne deepe insight, do very hardely suffer oure selves to be persuaded, that in matters of god [*sic*] it is utterly blynde and dull.[22]

Here the good reader's ears should twitch. We have been here before. If our insight is thus depraved, our reasoning is vain, and, if our reasoning is vain, our theology is vain. What then of the *Institutes* – a work of reason from beginning to end? The Calvinist answer is distressingly simple. The *Institutes* was not written by Calvin; it was written by God. This answer, so far from being extravagant, would be accepted, with downcast eyes and a modest smile, by Calvin himself. Remember the divine stanzas in Herbert. We asked, did Herbert write this material, or did God? Already that question should seem less wild.

The doctrine grows, then, from Paul and Augustine, especially from that in Augustine which was anti-Pelagian. It is difficult for the modern reader to understand the consistency and intensity of Protestant opposition to Pelagius. The man himself (especially if one has just been reading Calvin) seems luminously sane. Certainly the opposition hardened at the Reformation. Earlier Roman Catholic censure had been moderate, qualified at many points by respect for that in Pelagius

---

[21] ibid., II. ii. 11; in Norton's translation, fol. 10 *verso*.
[22] ibid., II. ii. 18, 19; fol. 13 *recto*.

which is pellucidly just (the proceedings of the Synod of Arles are highly informative). Pelagius held that men are capable of good, that spiritual effort was therefore necessary and desert possible. Like Dostoevsky's Grand Inquisitor, he thought that for God to ask more of man than man could perform was monstrous, but unlike the Inquisitor he drew the conclusion that God must have given man the necessary strength and discernment. This is the doctrine which Protestant writers, almost to a man, treat as a grotesque superstition. As Patrick Grant has written,[23] the Thirty-nine Articles, the Augsberg Confession, the Statements of Carnesecchi all tell the same, anti-Pelagian tale. The contempt is automatic yet ferocious and (this must be said) unintelligible to the author of this book. Augustine remorselessly opposed Pelagius's view that man might be capable of good. Yet, to Calvin, Augustine was not anti-Pelagian enough. Luther's bizarre contention that God wants us to sin is mirrored in Calvin in a form which is clearly anti-Pelagian:

> And there was no necessitie to compell God to geve him any other than a meane will and a fraile will, that of mans fall he myghte gather matter for his owne glory.[24]

It may be thought that we could hardly be further from the loving, other-directed God of Herbert.

Certainly Herbert could never state the doctrine in its full Calvinist clarity. He remains sure that, although God hates sin, he loves the sinner, and the strangely bleak triumph over evil we find in Calvin becomes in Herbert an altogether more mysterious victory of love over hate *within* the mind of God: 'Notwithstanding his infinite hate of sinne, his love overcame that hate, and with an exceeding great victory.'[25] Yet even Herbert's God can, for example, revel in the exercise of naked, capricious power in order to subject and terrify his creatures:

> God delights to have men feel, and acknowledg, and rever-
> ence his power, and therefore he often overturnes things

[23] *The Transformation of Sin*, p. 31.
[24] *Institutes*, I. xv. 8, fol. *verso*.
[25] *A Priest to the Temple* (1652), chap XXXIV, in *Works*, p. 283.

when they are thought past danger; that is his time of inter-
posing. As when a Merchant hath a ship come home after
many a storme which it hath escaped, he destroyes it some-
times in the very Haven. . . . If a farmer should depend upon
God all the yeer, and being ready to put hand to sickle,
shall then secure himself, and think all cock-sure; then God
sends such weather as lays the corn, and destroys it: or if he
depend upon God further, even till he imbarn his corn, and
then think all sure; God sends a fire, and consumes all that he
hath.[26]

All this is done that men may 'fear continually'.[27] Meanwhile it
is evident from Herbert's poetry that he adheres to the view
that all virtue lies with God, but of course the poems show us
the doctrine only as it applies to Herbert himself, where it
might be thought that personal modesty might influence theo-
logy. In fact, however, Herbert's notes on the *One Hundred
and Ten Considerations* of Juan de Valdes make two things
clear: first that Herbert fully accepted the Protestant doctrine
of divine grace and, second, that he was nevertheless obscurely
troubled by it. De Valdes (1500–41) was a Spaniard and (of
course) a Roman Catholic, but was strongly drawn to stress the
importance of faith as against works in the economy of salva-
tion. He exercised a crucial influence on Carnesecchi (who was
to be both beheaded and burned for his Lutheran heresies). The
*One Hundred and Ten Considerations* was itself suppressed by
the Spanish Inquisition. In his 'Sixth Consideration' de Valdes
drew a distinction between natural and acquired depravity and
asserted that man might by his own powers free himself from
the latter. Evidently he had moved only part of the way
towards Calvin's position. Herbert in response is flustered, and
generates a whole series of hasty distinctions. Certainly, he
says, both 'actual' sins and 'original' sins can be removed only
by grace; indeed, there may be another category of behaviour
consisting of habits, and this in turn may be subdivided into
'habits opposed to the theological virtues' and 'habits opposed
to the moral virtues'; the first (once more) can be cleared only

[26] ibid., chap. xxx, p. 271.
[27] ibid., p. 271.

by grace and, as for the other sort, while it is true that Pagans before the birth of Christ succeeded in suppressing such ill habits, they were able to do so 'only by the general Providence of God'.[28] 'Generall Providence', it would appear, is equivalent to Calvin's 'common grace', which would seem to leave man with precisely nothing which he can do 'of himself'. On other occasions, de Valdes is almost too strong a Protestant for Herbert, but in such places Herbert gives a sort of troubled assent. For example, de Valdes urges that God's will operates both directly and indirectly through human agents: 'Neither Pharaoh nor Judas, nor those who are *vessels of wrath* could cease to be such.' Herbert comments, 'This doctrine however true in substance, yet needeth discreet, and wary explaining.'[29] But the prior doctrine, that we can do nothing good, commands his ready assent: if the priest is thanked for his charity, he must direct those that thank him to glorify God, 'so that the thanks may go the right way, and thither onely, where they are onely due'.[30]

These, then, are the extremes of Protestantism. Man's nature is totally depraved and he can never deserve salvation. Any good we may seem to do is really God's work, not ours. *Sponte enim peccamus*, says Calvin in his commentary on Paul's Epistle to the Romans, *quia peccatum non esset, nisi voluntarium*, 'We sin of our own accord, for, if the sin were not voluntary, it would be no sin.'[31] *Certum enim est*, says Calvin in his homily on I Samuel 2, *hominem non posse libero suo arbitrio sese ad virtutem erigere ac componere*, 'It is certain that man cannot of his own free will raise himself up and dispose himself to virtue'.[32] We are free to sin but not to do good, and so we are not really free at all. And, of course, we are predestined to eternal damnation. At this most dreadful of doctrines Calvin himself paused in his Latin with the famous shudder – *Decretum quidem horribile fateor*, 'It is a terrible

---

[28] 'Briefe Notes on Valdesso's *Considerations*', *Works*, p. 308.
[29] ibid., p. 314.
[30] *A Priest to the Temple*, chap. XII, *Works*, p. 245.
[31] *Ioannis Calvini opera quae supersunt omnia*, ed. G. Baum, E. Cunitz, E. Reuss, vol. XLIX, Braunschweig, 1892, cols. 128–9.
[32] ibid., vol. XXIX, col. 308.

decree, I grant'.[33] Its basis is the old one; all is done for the sake of victory; grace alone can lift damnation; in damning all God provides himself with material on which his own grace may act. This grace is given only to some and never by desert.

In this theology we who are not Calvinists may detect one ray of light. As the face of God, the perfect, the all-glorious, grows steadily darker, the face of man grows – against the intention of the writer – slowly lighter. For Calvin can love this dreadful God. Someone in the universe can love someone other than himself and even love (remember the words of Christ) his enemy. Of course we can only make this point by ignoring one element in Calvinism, namely that which teaches us that, if Calvin's love of God is really good, it was God not Calvin who moved Calvin's will to love, so that the love of Calvin for God is in truth only another instance of the divine self-love – and the darkness drops again. But, as we shall see, the argument is rarely maintained with so much pertinacity; the sense persists that the universe is an arena in which God wins all the contests except one. The contest God loses is the moral contest, in which man, the humiliated, triumphs, as generosity morally transcends self-glorification. This, to be sure, is never openly confessed, but it is perceptible in the *Institutes* and grows clearer in the poetry of Herbert.

I have so far contented myself with giving the extremes (which are also the fundamentals) of Calvin's theology. This seemed the fairest course, since it is part of my thesis that Herbert's theology contains a powerful Calvinist element and I would not be thought guilty of evading the challenge implicit in such an assertion: can the sweet-natured country parson really have anything in him of the most terrible of theologians? If I were to confine myself to the periphery of Calvinism considered as a distinctive theology, if I were never to venture outside the platitudes of common Christianity and were to make *them* the basis of my link between Calvin and Herbert, I should have demonstrated nothing. But if the hard doctrines can be shown to be common to both, something will have been achieved.

[33] *Institutes*, III. xxiii. 7; in Norton's translation, fol. 251 *recto*.

To historians of this period there will be nothing novel in the claim that Calvinism is still strong in the poetry of Herbert. It has long been recognized that, just as Whitgift was *theologically* as much a Calvinist as Cartwright, so thirty years later Arminians found no difficulty in subscribing to Articles ix–xviii. Andrewes and Laud stressed free will, not from the Pelagian motive of finding scope for merit, but in order to emphasize human responsibility for evil, to show that damnation is really deserved and the action of grace thereby the greater. Even Hooker says that man can of himself do nothing meritorious.[34] Nicholas Ferrar was tolerant of Roman Catholics and included a cross in his church furnishings, but his *theology* was firmly Protestant. His admiration for the Roman Catholic theologian Juan de Valdes actually confirms this view, since, as we have seen, de Valdes was himself for faith, not works, and laboured to reconcile Catholic Spain to Lutheranism.[35]

Such was the hey-day of Calvinism. Of its decay after two centuries we have a haunting picture, in George Crabbe's *The Parish Register*. There we are told of a mild young man from Cambridge, who fell prey to a 'clamorous sect' of late-born Calvinists; the effect on his preaching was immediate:

'Conviction comes like lightning', he would cry;
'In vain you seek it, and in vain you fly;
'Tis like the rushing of the mighty wind,
Unseen its progress, but its power you find;
It strikes the child ere yet its reason wakes;
His reason fled, the ancient sire it shakes.
The proud, learn'd man, and him who loves to know
How and from whence these gusts of grace will blow,
It shuns, – but sinners in their way impedes,
And sots and harlots visits in their deeds:
Of faith and penance it supplies the place;

---

[34] 'A Learned Discourse of Justification', in *The Works of . . . Richard Hooker*, arranged by John Keble, 7th edn, revised by R. W. Church and F. Paget, 1888, vol. III, p. 493. See also W. H. Halewood, *The Poetry of Grace*, pp. 36–7.

[35] See Grant, *The Transformation of Sin*, pp. 34f.

Assures the vilest that they live by grace,
And, without running, makes them win the race.'
   Such was the doctrine our young prophet taught;
And here conviction, there confusion wrought;
When this thin cheek assumed a deadly hue,
And all the rose to one small spot withdrew:
They call'd it hectic; 'twas a fiery flush,
More fix'd and deeper than the maiden blush;
His paler lips the pearly teeth disclosed,
And lab'ring lungs the length'ning speech opposed.
No more his span-girth shanks and quiv'ring thighs
Upheld a body of the smaller size;
But down he sank upon his dying bed,
And gloomy crotchets fill'd his wandering head. –
   'Spite of my faith, all-saving faith,' he cried,
'I fear of wordly works the wicked pride;
Poor as I am, degraded, abject, blind,
The good I've wrought still rankles in my mind;
My alms-deeds all, and every deed I've done,
My moral-rags defile me, every one;
It should not be – what say'st thou? tell me, Ralph.'
Quoth I, 'Your reverence, I believe, you're safe;
Your faith's your prop, nor have you pass'd such time
In life's good-works as swell them to a crime.
If I of pardon for my sins were sure,
About my goodness I would rest secure.'[36]

   I have called this decay, but of course it is also growth. When
that poor confused man spoke of the mighty gale of unreason
he did little to revive Calvinism but something perhaps for the
gathering momentum of romanticism. These things never
really die.

[36] *Poems*, ed. A. W. Ward, Cambridge, 1905, pp. 221–2.

# IV

# HERBERT TESTS CALVIN

D'ou vient ceste affection de le prier? N'est-ce pas de son sainct Esprit?
Car jamais l'homme n'aura son recours a Dieu de son propre mouve-
ment.[37]

\*    \*

IN HIS Dedication Herbert wrote,

Lord, my first fruits present themselves to thee,
Yet not mine neither, for from thee they came. . . .

These are the first words of *The Temple*, as it was published in
1633, and already the theology is utterly radical. Indeed, by the
second line, Herbert is concerned to stress, not just the fierce
simplicity of the original doctrine (that all the good we do is
God's) but also its sheer strangeness, its mind-breaking awk-
wardness. The implication is that, if praying is good, God must
be praying to God (awkward, since it is man who needs to
pray) and God must be praising God (awkward, since Herbert
would have liked to do this). Let us hear no more of the serene
and tranquil country parson.[38] Herbert's thoughts are indeed,
as he says himself, 'a case of knives'. Even something as appar-
ently simple as a humble dedication cuts itself to pieces before
our eyes, as the humility of Herbert gives ground before the
self-glorification of God. The same radicalism can be seen in
*The Holdfast*:

Nay, ev'n to trust in him was also his:
We must confesse that nothing is our own.

Again he stresses the most awkward – in a way, the most
absurd – implication of the doctrine. If all virtue is God's, then
the virtue of trusting God must be God's. But, of course, some
actions are only virtues when performed by one in a subordi-

[37] Calvin, Sermon LXIX on Job 19; in *Opera*, vol. XXXIV, 1887, p. 100.
[38] For a good specimen of this powerful critical tradition, see C. V. Wedgwood,
*Seventeenth Century English Literature*, 1950, p. 83.

nate position. Just as it was man who *needed* to pray, so it is only man who might have done something deserving by trusting God. To trust one's own omnipotence is quite another matter. The wholesale transference of virtues to God turns out to imply the extinction of some of them. Yet the inference from Augustine and Calvin is logically impeccable. We may compare with the lines from the Dedication and *The Holdfast* the following: 'Thou art my grief alone' (*Affliction II*), *O dulcissime Spiritus,/Sanctos qui gemitus mentibus inseris*, 'O sweetest Spirit, who dost sow groanings in our hearts' (*Ad Deum, Musae Responsoriae, XL*) 'My heart did heave, and there came forth, O God!/By that I knew that thou wast in the grief' (*Affliction III*). In the last, quite clearly, God prays to God and Herbert stands aside in modest gratitude. Lest there be any doubt, prayer is defined by Herbert as 'Gods breath in man returning to his birth' (*Prayer I*). The image is very beautiful but at the same time obscurely troubling. Most of us prefer fresh air to $CO_2$.

The self-paralysing doctrine that human reason is futile likewise finds uncompromising expression:

> We say amisse,
> This or that is:
> Thy word is all if we could spell.
>
> (*The Flower*)

We may compare with this *Redemption*, a marvellously weird poem, the weirdness being at once dreamlike and technically Calvinist. It is most potent in the strange prolepsis of the last line

> Having been tenant long to a rich Lord,
>     Not thriving, I resolved to be bold,
>     And make a suit unto him, to afford
> A new small-rented lease, and cancell th' old.
> In heaven at his manour I him sought:
>     They told me there, that he was lately gone
>     About some land, which he had dearly bought
> Long since on earth, to take possession.
> I straight return'd, and knowing his great birth,
>     Sought him accordingly in great resorts;

> In cities, theatres, gardens, parks, and courts:
> At length I heard a ragged noise and mirth
> Of theeves and murderers: there I him espied,
> Who straight, *Your suit is granted*, said, & died.

Calvinism really implies the futility of prayer. So here the suit is granted *before* any request has been made. That this loving anticipation should be instantly followed by those bare monosyllables of thunderous import, 'said, & died' makes this one of the most sheerly exciting lines in all religious poetry.

Indeed, Calvin's God should be glad to have such a poet on his side, for it is the poetry that protects him here. Calvin's gross image of the divine landlord who wishes to protect his investment is made, most tenderly, to seem provisional and tentative here. Behind the thin, poor conception, we are made to sense the presence of some unimaginable love, sweetness, splendour, which forthwith submits to die in squalor for our sake.

Did Herbert believe that he himself might be predestined to eternal damnation?

> Whether I flie with angels, fall with dust,
> Thy hands made both, and I am there:
> Thy power and love, my love and trust
> Make one place ev'ry where.

(*The Temper I*)

It is as if he dare not speak clearly. 'Flie with angels' is an image of aspiration rather than of triumphant achievement. The phrase echoes that used by Horatio over the dead Hamlet, 'Flights of angels sing thee to thy rest' (v.ii.352). Even Horatio's generous spirit ventures only to hope for rather than to confide in the salvation of his friend (involved, as Hamlet is, in all the ambiguities of death). Herbert, for his own very different reasons, discovers a similar need for restraint. Where does faith end and presumption begin? Nevertheless, with all these reservations, 'flie with angels' is likely to refer to something more than some temporary exaltation of the spirits; the implied terminus of such a flight is surely Heaven itself. The other half of the antithesis, 'fall with dust', confirms the presentiment that Herbert is thinking of his own death. Remember here the thunderous conclusion of Izaak Walton's *Life of Dr Donne*:

> ... that body, which once was a Temple of the Holy Ghost,
> and is now become a small quantity of Christian dust.
> But I shall see it reanimated.[39]

Behind Walton's words are the words of the Psalmist, 'My soul
cleaveth to the dust. Quicken me' (Psalms 119: 25). Mean-
while, in the language of the New Testament, 'life' again and
again means salvation. The dead are raised up but not necessar-
ily to life:

> Marvel not at this: for the hour is coming, in which all that
> are in the graves shall hear his voice, and shall come forth;
> they that have done good, unto the resurrection of life; and
> they that have done evil, unto the resurrection of damnation.
>
> (John, 5: 28–9)

Thus, despite the doctrine of universal resurrection, the word
'death', in virtue of its opposition to 'life', continues to be used,
is given a special eschatological application and comes to mean
'damnation': 'The wages of sin is death, but the gift of God is
eternal life through Jesus Christ our Lord' (Romans, 6: 23).
'Dust' implies mortality, and mortality, especially when joined
with the idea of falling, implies damnation. No Protestant
reader, with the consequences of a 'fall from grace' still ringing
in his ears from the last sermon he heard, could avoid this
inference. If the muffled language has an effect, it is to make the
terror greater. Herbert knows that God may have damned him
and, in an agony of generous love, seeks to welcome even that
fact.

Here is strong meat – too strong, indeed, for the anonymous
adapter of 1697, who in his re-working of the poem chose to
omit this last stanza.[40] It remains just possible that 'fall with

---

[39] *The Lives of John Donne, Sir Henry Wotton, Richard Hooker, George
Herbert and Robert Sanderson*, with an introduction by George Saintsbury,
1927, p. 84.
[40] See Helen Vendler, *The Poetry of George Herbert*, Cambridge, Mass., 1975,
p. 40. Ms Vendler does not suggest that the stanza was omitted because of its
extreme theology, but the supposition is not improbable. In 1697 these lines
would have immediately suggested Quietism. The condemnation of Molinos
was recent history; the great Bossuet was in that very year sharpening his
arguments against Madame Guyon and Fénelon.

dust' refers not to damnation but merely to depression of spirits. I have argued against this interpretation, but, even if we accept it, it makes little difference, for to the Protestant mind such depression implies nothing less than damnation. Calvinism is a perfect instrument whereby both neurotic euphoria and neurotic depression can automatically intensify themselves. The fact that Herbert can so far subdue his fear of presumption as to envisage exaltation among the angels strongly suggests that thoughts of desert have been largely set aside. The fundamentalism of the last lines is staggering. In them he faces what Calvin shrank from: that God made hell, that unity with his will makes all places one, that hell is a suburb of the Heavenly City. Here, once more, let us imagine God reading. May we imagine that, as he reads, he is shamed?

This theology is, strictly speaking, unendurable. I mean by this that no one can bear to believe it steadily and consistently. Certainly Calvin could not.

To begin with, Protestant theology implies antinomianism (now we say it). When Luther says that God wants sinners, he adds that the expression, 'a holy man', is a contradiction in terms:

> It is a fictitious expression to speak of a 'holy man' . . . for by the nature of things this cannot be.
>
> For this reason we must reject those very ancient and deep-rooted errors by which in monastic fashion we speak of Jerome or Paul as 'holy'. In themselves they are sinners, and only God is holy. . . . As Peter is holy, so I am holy. As I am holy, so the thief on Christ's right hand is holy. It does not matter that Peter and Paul did greater things than you or I.[41]

Halewood, in *The Poetry of Grace*, is too bland in his easy acceptance of all this. He writes that Herbert 'is a moral poet only in "The Church Porch", on the other side of the wall from "The Church", which treats the urgent questions of God and man' (p. 96). This is at one and the same time technically correct and absurd. As if Herbert could ever cease to be a moral poet! With Herbert, as with Calvin, morality will 'keep break-

---

[41] Exposition of Psalm 51, in *Luther's Works*, vol. XII, p. 325.

ing in'. In the first impetus of his argument Calvin seems happily to concede that morality has simply vanished from the face of the earth, in so far as we are fallen (and we are fallen). He writes, of 'the philosophers':

> This principle they helde, that man could not be a livyng creature, endued with reason, unlesse there were in hym a free choise of good and evill: and they considered, that otherwise all the difference should be taken away between vertues and vices, unlesse man dyd order his own lyfe by his owne advise. Thus farre had they said well, if there had been no chaunge in man, which chaunge because they knowe not of, it is no marvaile though they confounde heaven and earthe togyther. . . . And there was no necessitie to compell God to geve him any other than a meane will and a fraile will, that of mans fall he myghte gather matter for his owne glory.[42]

We may set with this clear concession that the distinction between vice and virtue is applicable only to unfallen man, that other passage, already noticed, in which Calvin praises Augustine for seeing that, of himself, man is Satan. Yet immediately afterwards, Calvin commends humility and resignation, as attitudes proper to the circumstances. 'Proper' is here quite clearly a *moral* term. If resignation is better, more virtuous than rebellion (and on what other ground could it be commended?) some moral scope is after all left to man. But that in turn means that the original postulate of moral inefficacy, on which the injunction to be humble was based, is itself wrong! The good reader of Herbert should find all this familiar.

Sometimes, indeed, Calvin seems simply to be confused. The doctrine of man's total depravity, contemplated separately, would seem to imply the futility of all human thought and action and thus to mean, in particular, that, say, the science of Pasteur, the theology of Augustine and the logic of Aristotle are all equally erroneous. But there is, of course, another arm to the argument: God interpenetrates the universe and, wherever there is good, he is its agent. A little reflection will show that we

---

[42] *Institutes*, I. xv. 8; in Norton's translation, fol. 56 *recto, verso*.

now have a metaphysical doctrine so elastic as to 'save all the appearances'. Indeed, with a little conceptual adjustment, we might all grow quite cheerful and begin to remark how splendid (that is, how 'God-filled') a creature man is, he can do such clever things. Calvin never adjusts his mind so far, seemingly because he has an abiding appetite for gloom. But even he begins to wince a little at the sheer absurdity of total depravity:

> In this perverted and degendred nature of manne, there shiyne yet some sparkes that shewe that hee ys a creature havinge reason, and that hee differeth from brute beastes, bicause he is endued with understanding. . . .[43]

This, it might be thought, looks surprisingly like common sense. The phrase has hardly risen in the mind when we find Calvin explicitly deferring to its authority:

> So to condemne it i.e., human understanding of perpetual blyndenesse, that a man leave unto it no manner of skyll in any kynde of thynges, ys not onely agaynste the worde of God, but also agaynste the experience of common reason.[44]

Norton writes 'common reason', but Calvin wrote *sensus communis*. Calvin's best modern translator, Ford Lewis Battles, naturally, writes 'common sense'.

Is this Calvinism? Calvin says it, but it is not Calvinism. Within three pages, the radical theology begins to kick back, using the only means open to it. At first we seem still to be in the ordinary, chatty world of common sense:

> Shal we saye that they were madde, whiche in settynge fourthe Physycke, have employed theyr dilygence for us? What of all the mathematicall sciences? shall wee thynke them dotynge erroures of madde menne?[45]

But then the answer begins to come through. These gleams of competence are part of our nature, it is true, and thus can be provisionally contrasted with the special illuminations of

---

[43] ibid., II. ii. 12; fol. 10 *verso*.
[44] ibid., II. ii. 12; fol. 10 *verso*.
[45] ibid., II. ii. 15; fol. 12, *recto*.

( *38* )

Grace. But then God is equally the author of our nature (and so the antithesis dissolves) and his creative efficacy is not something belonging to the remote past but a present reality:

> It is no marvel if the knowledg of those thinges whiche are moste excellent in mans life, be sayde to be communicated unto us by the spirite of God. Neither is there cause why any manne should aske, what have the wicked to doe with Gods spirite, whiche are altogether estranged from God. For where it is saide that the spirite of God dwelleth in the faythfull onely, that is to be understanded of the spyrite of santification, by the whyche we are consecrate to God him selfe, to be his temples: yet doeth he nevertheless fyll, move and quicken all thynges. . . .[46]

It is clear that, although Calvin had begun by allowing some competence to human reason, that competence must upon reflection be ascribed, by the usual Augustinian logic, to God. That the theology of the *Institutes* itself is *a fortiori* the more certainly God's work is made clear at II.ii.20. J. T. McNeill comments, 'This assertion of the divine origin and authentification of "truth wherever it appears" could hardly be more emphatic.'[47] A little later he comments on Calvin's conception of special grace, which may enable a man to serve well in the world though he himself remain in a state of total depravity. It is not to be supposed, writes McNeill, that this form of grace 'has any relation to the salvation of the possessor'.[48]

The whole sequence is of great interest, both philosophical and psychological. It shows Calvin to have been sensitive to the *a posteriori* claims of common experience. He might have stuck more simply to his first position: 'Of course *you* think, from your point of view, that Pasteur was a great scientist; but have I not just explained that you and he, as human beings, are equally benighted?' Such might have been the way of the remoter sort of metaphysician, a Leibniz, say, or a Spinoza. But Calvin wants 'good', 'reason' and 'true' to mean what they ordinarily mean and this is to grant them at least the possibility

---

[46] ibid., II. ii. 16; fol. 12, *recto, verso*.
[47] In the Battles translation, p. 274 n.
[48] ibid., p. 276.

of ordinary application to the usual objects, in this world. The concession, as it shall appear, is crucial.

It has long been commonplace to observe that Calvinism, which implies the futility of moral effort, produced the most morally strenuous culture the world has ever seen. Those most drawn to Calvinism were those most easily engaged by moral questions, the scrupulous, the committed. By and large, the two incompatible requirements, that of rational consistency and that of moral urgency, owe their continued coexistence to an area of sustained confusion: though no work is meritorious, resignation, in a manner, is allowed to be so. But, in truth, whether we stress the pessimistic side of Calvin ('All men are damned') or the optimistic side ('but Christ redeems'), morality is extinguished. As we have seen, Calvin himself wavered. William Perkins, the great English Puritan, endeavoured somehow to make room for both man's moral irrelevance and his moral obligations, somewhat in the manner of a skilled Chairman of a Committee (such men are trained to suppress basic issues). In *A Reformed Catholike* Perkins wrote:

> In the very first instant of the conversion of a sinner, sinne receiveth his deadly wound in the root, never afterward to be recovered.[49]

But he also wrote, in *The Grain of Mustard Seed*, 'The fore-said beginnings of grace are counterfeit, unless they increase', and goes on to explain how the spark of grace may go out (here we should remember Herbert's *The Starre* and *Artillerie*, in both of which a spark comes down from Heaven) unless 'they labour to increase and go on from faith to faith'.[50]

It might be thought that, formally, there is no obvious contradiction in Perkins' reasoning. The first passage refers to renovation after it has been made perfect, the second to that crucial stage between the beginning of renovation and its completion; moral effort, rendered irrelevant by the first, is urgently necessary in the second. In fact, however, the first passage, from *A Reformed Catholike*, refers to baptism. Per-

[49] *The workes of . . . Mr. William Perkins*, 3 vols, Cambridge 1616–18, vol. I, p. 562.
[50] ibid., p. 642.

kins is labouring to refute the claim that Protestantism removes the efficacy of baptism, by making it a mere pruning rather than an extirpation of sin. He is in real difficulty and his flurry of distinctions, as between the guilt of sin, removed by baptism, and the corruption of nature, at first unchanged by baptism,[51] cannot really help him. In any case, by strict Calvinist theology moral effort is irrelevant at all times. In a similarly equivocal manner, Perkins argues that though the godly commit the same sins as the ungodly, they do not *consent* to them as the ungodly do.[52] Clearly, he is trying to find a way of reassuring the good Puritan that he is in fact more *meritorious* than his drunken neighbour, though the word itself can never be used. And at all times there remains, in both Augustine and Calvin, a carefully preserved ambiguity in the concept of *will*.

To start with, the notion that God may move a man's *will* is already at least puzzling and, at most, contradictory. Will is, *ex hypothesi*, self-moving. If it is moved by some external force (this does not apply, of course, to teleological causation, that is, to a good *reason* beckoning the mind from in front) it is no longer will. A man whose 'will' is moved from behind to do something is, quite simply, a man who is made to do something; he may think he willed it, but really he did not. In such circumstances, all talk of will is mere obfuscation and should be cut short. But, of course, in the psychological experience of such determinate actions the illusion of willing can be potent, and it is here that a theologian, anxious to preserve a sense in the subject that, even if he is capable of no good act, he is nevertheless responsible for the evil he does, may pitch his tent. But it is best to begin with Augustine:

> The mind commands the hand to be moved; and such readiness is there, that command is scarce distinct from obedience. Yet the mind is mind, the hand is body. The mind commands the mind, its own self, to will, and yet it doth not. Whence this monstrousness? and to what end? It commands

<hr>

[51] See *A Golden Chaine*, *Workes*, vol. I, p. 98. This conflict in Perkins' thought was pointed out to me by Mr Adrian Pinnington.

[52] *A Treatise tending to a Declaration whether a Man be in the Estate of Damnation*, *Workes*, vol. I, 372.

itself, I say, to will and would not command unless it willed, and what it commands is not done.[53]

This is marvellously acute. Here Augustine challenges Descartes across the centuries, and at the same time his imagination reaches out to Marlowe's Faustus and Shakespeare's Claudius, each of whom struggles to bend his own will to repentance. Indeed, the echoes of Augustine's thought may even extend as far as the strange hero of Dostoevsky's *Notes from Underground*, a creature whose every other action is paralysed by excess of consciousness. What Augustine has done is to analyse, as a matter of observable psychological fact, the possible reduplications of the will. In a way the word 'abstraction' would be appropriate here, so long as it were made clear that the abstraction in question is not logical but psychological. Man may will a thing and do it. Or he may will a thing and not do it. Or he may will to will a thing – and not do it.

We have then in this passage from the *Confessions* a closely observed regression which may be compared with the moral regression of a Herbert poem. In Herbert, the praying subject endeavours to deserve God's love by being good and then withdraws as he realizes that his effort to deserve is itself absurd, and then withdraws *again* as he realizes that his ostentatious waiving of desert might itself be construed as a covert assertion of merit. The scheme is in principle indefinitely extendable. When Herbert does this, what we watch is the perennial struggle under Calvinism of the individual moral agent to find some territory – though it prove of ever-diminishing extent – to call his own. So in Augustine, the ever less potent will is, in his example, a will to a good, made bodily manifest in the world, and yet at the same time it seems ever more poignantly cut off from the world, more ineffectually personal. That in the organism which fails to perform seems 'further out', less personal, than that which still wishes to be good. Thus the suggestion is planted that that which wills to will, though absurdly impotent, is not itself corrupt. Thus, in this dual conception of the will, we find a sort of mitigation of the total depravity of human nature. Inside every depraved

[53] *Confessions*, VIII. ix. 21.

(42)

nature is an ineffectual angel. This particular doctrine finds no significant followers in the seventeenth century. But the more general intuition, bequeathed by Augustine, that the will is not a simple thing, that there may be a duplicity in willing, whereby a man may at the same time will and not will – this provided Calvin with a foundation on which he could build:

> For if we be holden bounde of oure owne luste wherein sinne reighneth, so that we are not loose at libertie to obey oure father, there is no cause why we shoulde allege necessitie for oure defense, the evell whereof is bothe within us, and to be imputed unto oure selves.[54]

In effect, the psychological scheme proposed by Augustine has been turned inside out and projected upon the cosmos. In the process the ethical character of what is done is reversed. Augustine pointed out how the more personal will could try (albeit ineffectually) to move the less personal will. Calvin points out how the will of God is able (only too effectually) to move the will of man to evil (by giving him a certain nature) and yet it is man's will which culpably completes the last stage, that is, the actual performance of evil. How many modern readers are aware that the doctrine of imputed righteousness is answered, in Calvin, by a doctrine of imputed evil?

What Augustine's psychological analysis does is to drive a wedge into the gross simplicity of our first formulation: 'will is *ex hypothesi* self-moving'. He seemed to show that will *itself* could be not only the subject but also the object of motion – or, at least, the object of a would-be mover – in those odd but perfectly recognizable situations in which 'we will to will'. But if the will can be so moved and still be will, Calvin joyously reasons, evil may be at one and the same time ours and 'imputed to us'. The whole exercise is a piece of sophistry, at first brilliant, at last merely brutal. For if we were to succeed in our willing to will, the second of those wills can no longer be true volition but must rather be desire. But, of course, we do not succeed. The experience of 'willing to will' is, as the later poetry of Eliot teaches us, naturally an experience of incapacity

---

[54] *Institutes*, II. viii. 2; fol. 45 *verso*.

(43)

and not of triumphant self-government. Thus a degree of spontaneity remains with the second 'will' (that which the first will is striving to move). And so the second will may indeed be seen as genuinely volitional, precisely because it is *not* wholly subject to an external mover. Note that in Calvin's scheme this does not hold. The determinations of God are infallible and irresistible. Therefore the attempt of the Calvinist to claim freedom for an imputed will is ill-judged. Calvin himself is usually willing to recognize this.

With Herbert there is no such overt attempt as we find in Perkins to smuggle human morality into the theory of his religion. It is rather the *practice* of morality which endlessly insinuates itself, for in the darkened Garden of Calvinism the serpent's name is Virtue. Herbert will try to be good and this he knows is presumption. It is one of the earlier triumphs of Calvinism to make virtue a mode of sin. Thus we find in his poems that strange impulse to engage in moral competition with God which Helen Vendler has noted.[55] In *The Thanksgiving* he explicitly recognizes this and tries to deal with it.

> Surely I will revenge me on thy love,
>   And trie who shall victorious prove.
> If thou dost give me wealth, I will restore
>   All back unto thee by the poore.
> If thou dost give me honour, men shall see,
>   The honour doth belong to thee.

But, of course, all this must be repented and recanted by the close of the poem, and indeed Herbert seems to bring it off most beautifully. The proposed contest with God's goodness grows more and more phrenetic as each of God's gifts is matched until we reach the last:

> Then for thy passion – I will do for that –
>   Alas, my God, I know not what.

And God's victory is sealed. But here we must ask our running question: sealed by whom? Why, by George Herbert. And this realization gives birth to a further presentiment: why, then, the

---

[55] *The Poetry of George Herbert*, p. 233.

competition is still running and perhaps George Herbert has won after all. Herbert himself would doubtless deny this strenuously; he wrote secure in the knowledge that *he* had not endured crucifixion and this is enough to ensure the dominance of Christ at the end. Nevertheless, the situation which Herbert has allowed to become clear is fraught with peril. Though Herbert had no fears that he might rival Christ's Passion, certain martyrs of the Church, in terms of physical pain, must have done just that. St Peter, in fear of this, desperately devised for himself the bizarre and artificial humiliation of an inverted crucifixion. But even while Christ's sacrifice burns in the mind we notice that here the final act of generosity and abnegation is Herbert's. We all know that in the moral competitions which are running at all times in most families, final concession of a point can be a mode of victory. But, of course, if that is so and the fact is noticed, the whole game is to be played again. In so far as Herbert has finally established his own unselfishness (while Christ's very passion according to Calvin, was done to please himself) it might be thought that after all he has won. But if he realizes this, he will know that in another game he has lost; for, once more, he has presumed. Herbert is involved in an infinite regress, of a singularly strenuous kind. As soon as we allow any virtue or merit to the last, sobbing line of the poem, the theological difficulty is upon us. And if we break the ontological circle of the poem and ask, 'Who stage-manages this defeat for Herbert?' the difficulties become insuperable. The so-called 'resolutions' of Herbert are often as implictly explosive as this.

It is perhaps worth noticing that in *The Thanksgiving* it is virtually impossible to ascribe the 'virtue' shown by the Herbert figure to God himself. To do so is to make God compete with himself in just those good works which Calvinism habitually disparages and would turn the final gesture of submission on Herbert's part into an almost unintelligible, peculiarly exacerbated form of divine self-respect, conducted through a human subject. Remember the words uttered by Herbert in the first euphoria of the contest: 'I'll build a spittle', that is, an hospital. This brief design is soon left far behind in the spiritual wake of the poem. Let us vary our method and make not God but the sick into eavesdroppers on the poem's progress. They will soon perceive that they are after all in for a long wait. Building operations are not really in hand.

Consider next *Affliction I*. The poem begins with what might, from another poet, have been a conclusion: the poet describes his joy on being claimed by God. The emotion and the attitude are both, as we say today, entirely 'sympathetic'. The lines look like the purest piety. Herbert tells us how in his youthful innocence he sought God's face and at first God gave him, if not the sight of his countenance, at least great happiness:

> My dayes were straw'd with flow'rs and happinesse;
> There was no moneth but May.

But this happiness was soon curtailed, first by mental distress and then by physical pain. God did all of this. Then, as the poet's health returned, God began to kill his friends. His next action, happily, is more forgivable. Instead of packing Herbert off, where his natural temper and social rank would have made him happy, to the Court, God sent him to Cambridge and kept him there by 'the sweetn'd pill' of 'academick praise'. This moment is interesting because it shows how far Herbert is prepared to go in imputing to God the use of ostensibly immoral means, on the security of the reader's knowledge of God's profound goodness, always there in the background. But then, lest Herbert should be too 'happy' in his 'unhappiness', God visits him with more sicknesses. Here one begins to sense a real and acute resentment at the trick God played with the sweetened pill of academic praise. Note that Herbert here claims, quite seriously, to have seen through the trick God played on him and therefore is in a manner standing up to God. And now Herbert asks, not to be spared any of his pains, but to be allowed to be good and fruitful. He asks to be *virtuous*.

The pace has now grown warm. Herbert recoils momentarily and strives to extort from himself the proper expression of resignation:

> Yet I must be meek. . . .

At this point in the moral contest *The Thanksgiving* ends, by supplying an action of meekness. But in *Affliction I* the lid will not stay down.

Well, I will change the service, and go seek
  Some other master out.
Ah my deare God, though I am clean forgot!
Let me not love thee, if I love thee not.

There is no formal reconciliation at all. The poem ends in splinters and in unendurable love. He cannot be meek, if meekness means agreeing not to be good and fruitful; he would rather – he thinks for a moment – move his allegiance elsewhere. But then he finds that the goodness and fruitfulness he desires are inextricably bound up with his love of God and can exist in no other relation. And so he must stay, commit the sin of virtue which is one with the sin of love, even if it means God's displeasure.

The almost unintelligible, strangled repetition at the end is unique in Herbert. I take it that the wording reflects the verbal form of a curse: 'Let me go hang, if I do not love you!' But, by sheer pressure of the thought, the content of the curse is so to speak invaded by the content of his major moral fear: 'Let the *worst* happen to me, let me be stopped from loving you, if I . . . ever step loving you.' Remember that among the ungodly of the time such self-cursings were part of the ordinary fabric of strong asseveration: 'If I be not ashamed of my soldiers, I am a soused gurnet' (*Henry IV*, Part I, iv.ii.11). In the last agony of Herbert's poem, the reckless idioms of youth contend and join with the darker terrors of maturity. Do we not say today 'I'll be damned if I won't'?

In *Affliction I* the moral contest is played out with no more than the briefest hint of that modulation to the other key of submission which we find elsewhere. The onslaught of God is truly formidable; so formidable that one wonders how so many generations of pious readers can have read it without offence. Presumably Herbert relies on the unspoken assumption of God's real, overwhelming goodness. This, rather than any submission on *his* part, is the 'external corrective' of the poem. The one (unforgivable) alternative possibility is that Herbert *confides* in God's seeing this aspect of things so that he will at last applaud the proper reticence of this poem in which Herbert has austerely refrained from any moral intrusion on

God's prerogative! But in truth Herbert has risked much. Perhaps, in terms of Protestant theology, he has risked too much. For, if the separation between virtue and that which pleases God is complete, we may begin to ask, 'When then is God good?' We derive the content of the word *good* from human concerns and activities. Thus, when a Calvinist praises God for his loving generosity in redeeming worthless man, 'generosity' is necessarily construed by analogy with human acts of charity. We may of course choose to re-define *good* as meaning 'Whatever God does'. But any lexicographer would instantly relegate this (weird) meaning to a separate sense. Indeed, Calvin's God is so utterly transcendent as to be strictly indescribable in human language. But to say that he is indecribable has more, and more uncomfortable, implications than most people realize. It means, for example, that he is not good.

It is sometimes suggested that the logical uniqueness of God can be reconciled with a kind of poetic description of him if we invoke the doctrine of analogy: though God is clearly not an ordinary biological father we can nevertheless call him 'father' by analogy with biological paternity. In this example, however, certain latent terms, like 'source' and 'protector' are common to God and to earthly fathers and sustain the analogy from below. These terms are used as if they were literally applicable to God. Where there is no such common ground there can be no analogy. Bishop Berkeley made this admirably clear in his reply to Peter Browne of Trinity College, Dublin. 'Wise' and 'good', he affirmed, must be applied in exactly the same sense to God as to man; 'Otherwise, it is evident that every syllogism brought to prove those attributes, or (which is the same thing) to prove the being of God, will be found to consist of four terms, and consequently can conclude nothing.'[56] Berkeley's reference to a four-term syllogism perhaps requires explanation. Here is an ordinary three-term syllogism:

> All good beings are merciful.
> God is a good being.
> Therefore God is merciful.

[56] *Alciphron, or the Minute Philosopher*, iv. 22, in *The Works of George Berkeley*, ed. A. A. Luce and T. E. Jessop, vol. III, 1950, p. 171.

The manner in which this can be turned, by the doctrine of analogy, into a four-term syllogism can be seen in the following, altered version:

All good beings (as 'good' is ordinarily understood) are merciful.
God is a good being, but in a unique sense.
Therefore God is . . . ?

As Berkeley says, we can conclude nothing.

Thus Herbert's moral competition with Calvin's God appears increasingly to be a rash enterprise – the probability of winning is far too high. For if God is beyond human language, a contest in terms of human conceptions like goodness will naturally go to the human contestant. As William Perkins wrote, God's 'actions are not within the compasse of morall lawes, as mens are'.[57] Meanwhile, for those who cannot help applying ordinary judgements, a God who hates his creatures, predestines them to eternal damnation and loves them only in so far as they are his property and provide matter for a feat of redemption will appear quite simply evil. There is nothing anachronistic in the grounds advanced for this inference. They are, quite simply, that hatred, cruelty avarice and pride are wrong. What is anachronistic is the imprudent baldness of the argument, applied as it is to God himself. For, with all these pressing difficulties, it remained a *given* fact for most of them, as it does not for us, that God is good.

Now let us examine *Affliction IV*.

> Broken in pieces all asunder,
>     Lord, hunt me not,
>     A thing forgot,
> Once a poore creature, now a wonder,
>     A wonder tortur'd in the space
>     Betwixt this world and that of grace.
>
> My thoughts are all a case of knives,
>     Wounding my heart
>     With scatter'd smart,

[57] *An Exposition of the Creed*, *Workes*, vol. I, p. 160.

As watring pots give flowers their lives.
  Nothing their furie can controll,
  While they do wound and pink my soul.

All my attendants are at strife,
  Quitting their place
  Unto my face:
Nothing performs the task of life:
  The elements are let loose to fight,
  And while I live, trie out their right.

Oh help, my God! let not their plot
  Kill them and me,
  And also thee,
Who art my life: dissolve the knot,
  As the sunne scatters by his light
  All the rebellions of the night.

Then shall those powers, which work for grief,
  Enter thy pay,
  And day by day
Labour thy praise, and my relief;
  With care and courage building me,
  Till I reach heav'n, and much more, thee.

Notice, once again, the curiously egalitarian tone of this poem. Herbert seems really to seek to change the mind of God, in particular to persuade him to drop the policy of hunting, to call off the hound of Heaven. At line 21 he even suggests that the present policy may prove fatal, not just to George Herbert, but (most oddly) to God himself. Perhaps the meaning is: 'Kill the God in-dwelling in Herbert', but even so, that is sufficiently odd. For, unless Herbert has forgotten the previous stanzas, he must know that his pains were inflicted by God and not self-inflicted. Moreover, the title is clearly Jobian. So what is he saying? It must be something like, 'I do think you ought to stop all this; you may hurt not just me but yourself.' He then points out respectfully that the divine energies which now work destructively might usefully be combined harmoniously. Again we ask, how is God supposed to take this? Is he to scratch his head like Bertie Wooster and say, 'Good Lord, Jeeves, I never thought of that. You really are amazing'? In all sobriety, Herbert seems to be telling God how to do his job. Moreover the very moral elevation of the argument makes the insult to God all the more profound. The tone is almost rallying. 'Wouldn't it be better to make *fruitful* use of all this?' Sheer, self-interested pleading would smack more of humility, less of blasphemy. Yet if one is to persuade God, Herbert might say, would not moral reasons weigh more heavily with him than immoral? The answer is that of course they do; they *already* do — with their absolute weight. To propose to correct God on a moral point is to carry presumption to its utmost limit; unless, like Job, you do it in a sort of innocent passion.

But to be sure Herbert is very knowing. Perhaps (though this will seem oversubtle to most readers as it does to me) he knew that his prayer and his persuasion were absurd, but judged it more comely and more humble to incur the charge of presumption than to seek to evade it by a pretense of vulgar pleading. The paradox whereby virtue is sin and sin virtue will always permit these reversals (as it would permit, at a yet higher level of consciousness, yet another reversal, and so on *ad infinitum*). But I dare swear that no Anglican reader of Herbert has ever taken it so.

It will by now be evident that Herbert is an extremist. Far more than Donne, he subjects every insight to the test of extremity. But I would go further than this. I claim that the poetry of Herbert, once set upon this path, does more than its author ever intended it to do. Amongst other things, it pragmatically refutes the theology of Calvin. Calvin's God is subjected to love in the poetry of Herbert and is proved to be unloveable. Both arguments and poems have a life of their own. To take an example from another century, the question, 'What did Hume mean?' is quite different from the question, 'What does Hume's philosophy imply?' The sceptical arguments of the first two books of *The Treatise* are fatal to the psychologizing afterthoughts of the third book.[58] Hume himself either missed this or pretended not to know. As with Hume, so with Calvin. Modern commentators delight to point

[58] See my *A Common Sky*, 1974, p. 98.

out the moments of mitigating sanity in Calvin, his concession to natural theology, his awareness of human achievement. But Calvin had unleashed doctrines which nothing could withstand. He may speak of natural theology, but everyone who has digested the primary doctrine of human nature knows that natural theology is a contradiction in terms.

Meanwhile, Herbert trained himself in a certain mode of poetry, a mode having a law and a lawlessness, an *impetus* of its own. This mode, begun by Donne, consists chiefly in the practice of running arguments down, like hares, till they collapse in exhaustion. The curious thing is that the practice began as a sort of joke. Teachers of English quite properly instruct their students that the poets called 'Metaphysical' are not really so at all. They are not metaphysical as Dante or Wordsworth is metaphysical. Scholastic puzzles may appear in the poetry of Donne, but they are there to be played with and not as the vehicles of assertion. Similarly, technical theology appears more often in the sportive plane of metaphor than in the literal plane of Donne's poems. Theology is for love poems, where it will prove divertingly incongruous, just as erotic imagery is for religious poems ('nor ever chaste, except you ravish me'). The devotional poems themselves present, beneath the fireworks of metaphor, an anti-theological simplicity. Dame Helen Gardner draws our attention to Donne's own words: 'Morall Divinity becomes us all ... Metaphysick Divinity, almost all may spare.'[59] Such may have been the beginning of Metaphysical verse. The case has been presented with a false simplicity, for even in Donne one senses that in some poems a genuinely metaphysical theme is struggling for expression in, of all things, the hyperbolical-fantastical, Metaphysical mode; the *Nocturnall upon St Lucies Day*, the *Anniversaries*, *The Exstasie* all have this strange atmosphere of genuinely metaphysical thought somehow paraded in a 'Metaphysical' masquerade; it is as if one were to say, 'On the way home I was dogged by an Alsatian'. But in Herbert this sur-real incongruity vanishes. It vanishes because his *matter* is itself a thing of quite breathtaking extremes. The matter of Herbert's poetry, far

[59] See her edition of Donne's *Divine Poems*, 1952, p. xix.

more than the matter of Donne's, is a landscape of heights and precipices. We do not find in his poetry the fire and ice of Donne because his voice, unlike Donne's, is hushed before something far hotter than fire, far colder than ice:

Who straight, *Your suit is granted*, said, & died.

(*Redemption*)

Donne's poetry remains in a rhetorical limbo, and that is why the reader of the *Anniversaries* finds himself confused: 'Is this the end of the world, or not?' In Herbert the air clears, not by the abolition of extremes but, on the contrary, by our taking them straight. Herbert dispenses with hyperbole and instead embraces a doctrine far more precipitate than millenarian apocalypse; he embraces radical Calvinism. And the 'Metaphysical' mode continued, with a ferocity infinitely increased by the purgation of frivolity, to run down its arguments till they fell, exhausted.

It might be said that it is perverse to extract, with so much labour, an *implicit* condemnation of Calvinism from a poet who openly belonged to another party anyway; Luther may have considered the expression 'holy man' a contradiction in terms, but the Church to which Herbert belonged believed emphatically in saints, naming its places of worship after them and assigning them feast days. Was not Herbert's Church the Church of Andrewes and Laud? Doubtless there were many ways in which Herbert seriously dissented, with the support of his Church, from the teaching of Calvin, most notably perhaps in his doctrine of the Eucharist. But there was one tenet which he approached, not with hostility but with eager submission, and assigning them feast days. Was not Herbert's Church the doctrine is irreconcilable with the common Anglican regard for special saints of the Church. One is reminded of Alice's objection and the Dormouse's reply:

'They couldn't have done that, you know. They'd have been ill.'
'So they were, *very* ill.'

The confession of total depravity lies, inescapably, at the heart of Herbert's poems. He triumphs over it, not by expelling it

(53)

from his mind, but by applying to it the strange test of charitable belief.

Ironically (and yet naturally) Herbert's insistence on his own worthlessness was construed as evidence of sanctity, and so he emerges in Walton's *Life* as – that which the doctrine implicitly rules out – a kind of saint. Plato's piety to his dead teacher allowed or indeed compelled him to contradict his teaching; Socrates had claimed to know nothing and Plato credited him with a systematic metaphysical omniscience. George Herbert professed that he was worthless and Walton, more willing to trust in the man than in the generalized theology, thought it consistent with his piety to the memory of Herbert to find virtue in the very profession. If Calvin was right, Walton was wrong; more strangely, if Herbert was right, Walton was wrong.

I have put the case as it appears when traced in the vast and heady medium of warring theologies. But it can also be traced in minute particulars, even in something so lexically minute as Herbert's use of pronouns.

V

## HERBERT AND ENGLISH PRONOUNS

IN REAL use pronouns are more slippery things than one might expect and seem naturally to admit a certain latitude of abuse. Consider, for example, that very general feature of Chomskian psychology whereby so many languages pluralize 'thou' for the polite form, presumably because the singular is too intrusively particular, too like a dig in the ribs. But the impulse to lose the singular in a cloud of plurality occurs in other places and for other reasons – frequently, I think, unnoticed by grammarians. Look, for example, at the first word in Wyatt's celebrated lyric:

> They fle from me that sometyme did me seke
> With naked fote stalking in my chambre.
> I have sene theim gentill tame and meke

That nowe are wyld and do not remembre
That sometyme they put theimself in daunger
To take bred at my hand; and nowe they raunge
Besely seking with a continuell chaunge.

Thancked be fortune, it hath ben othrewise
Twenty tymes better; but ons in speciall
In thyn arraye after a pleasaunt gyse
When her lose gowne from her shoulders did fall,
And she me caught in her armes long and small;
Therewithall swetely did my kysse,
And softely said 'dere hert, how like you this?'

It was no dreme: I lay brode waking.
But all is torned thorough my gentilnes
Into a straunge fasshion of forsaking;
And I have leve to goo of her goodeness,
And she also to vse new fangilnes.
But syns that I so kyndely ame serued,
I would fain knowe what she hath deserued.

The grammar of this poem modulates from a plural to a singular pronoun, from 'they' to 'she'. This is commonly explained as an ordinary transition from a generic observation to a particular instance, which is indeed what 'they' followed by 'she' might be expected to mean. But I do not believe it. The reference throughout is, I suspect, to one girl. The initial 'they' has the effect of neutralizing a painfully pointed reference by distancing it, or perhaps it would be more accurate to say, by spreading it out. This strategem may be founded on a fact about human vision, namely that it is more difficult to focus on a number of things than on one. The use of 'they' I here attribute to Wyatt is not so common in English as to get into grammar books. It certainly is not current idiom. But it is not difficult to imagine how it might become so. We can easily imagine a world rather like ours in which people might say, 'They're giving me a bad time, you know. Do you know what she did last weekend?' That feels almost like current English to me. Latin poetry, which moves more freely between singular and plural than does English, can, I think, provide parallels.

For example, in the fourth book of the *Aeneid*, the shade of Mercury appears to the sleeping Aeneas and urges him to leave Carthage at once. Virgil then described the waking Aeneas in these words:

> Tum vero Aeneas, subitis exterritus umbris
> corripit e somno corpus

> Thereupon Aeneas, startled by the sudden ghosts
> wrenched his body from sleep.

Virgil writes, not *umbra* but *umbris*, not 'ghost' but 'ghosts'. A much more doubtful but, I think, really a more apposite example occurs in line 320 of the same book, where Dido says:

> Nomadumque tyrani
> odere

> The Numidian chieftains hate me

but as far as you can tell, she seems to be referring to only one person, Iarbas. Incidentally, if one is translating Wyatt's poem into French, the word to translate 'They' is 'On'.

Consider also the tendency, first of kings, and then of the authors of books to substitute 'we' for 'I'. Or else consider what might be called the Mary Poppins use of 'we', which really implies (though it does not profess) 'You as assimilated to my will' – 'Now we are feeling *much* jollier, aren't we?'

The purely linguistic slipperiness of pronouns, especially the second person, is rendered still more problematic by the supervening conventions, first of prayer and then of literature. In Homer, perhaps, the two are one. Homer's σύ ('thou') is never, I think, the reader or auditor, always the Muse. This is the more striking if we reflect that Homer may well have been an oral poet, a public performer. Yet he never addresses the people gathered round him. One wishes to say, 'his eyes are on another object' and at once one remembers the legend: Homer was blind. The poetry of Homer is the most pellucid ever written, and yet it is surprising how many of the problems one associates with seventeenth-century religious verse do in fact appear in it. For example, the question, 'Who creates the poem?' has the same provoking relevance. Both the *Iliad* and the *Odyssey* begin with an imperative of invocation; the Muse is asked to sing the wrath of Achilles or tell *the poet* (μοι; 'me') of the resourceful Odysseus. The poet sings then, ἐκ θεῶν, 'out of the gods'. Yet, if the Muse creates the poem, who created the exordium and invocation, itself linguistically one texture with the rest? Here alone, it may seem, the poet was truly poet or maker of his verse, for a ten-line space, before the Muse took over for the following twelve thousand lines? Of Herbert we asked 'If the poem comes from God, are we to suppose that God prays to God?' Just as we imagined Herbert praying before and on behalf of his flock, so we must imagine Homer, rapt in his inspiration and yet responsive to the least stirring of boredom in his human audience. Yet in Homer the problems remain securely buried beneath the poem's golden surface. He will never − could not conceivably − break that enigmatic simplicity of presentation. He will never sing words like:

My God, I mean my self

as Herbert does in *Miserie*.

Herbert's 'thou' nevertheless is, like Homer's, pretty safely insulated from any reference to the reader. Not for him the pseudo-frontal challenge of:

Hypocrite lecteur, − mon semblable, − mon frère.[60]

Even in Herbert's Dedication, where the reader is admitted to the suburbs of the poem, it is as the object of an imperative addressed to another. The readers remain in the third person, the second person remains God's:

Turn their eyes hither, who shall make a gain. . . .

But what happens when an artist does permit himself to *address* his reader? Once more the duplicity of literary pronouns does its strange work. Sterne, for example, is for ever prodding, cajoling and frustrating his reader, with a most unthrifty frequency of second person pronouns. Yet what grows from this is not a relation of real intimacy so much as a

---

[60] Baudelaire, 'Au Lecteur', *Les Fleurs du Mal*, in *Oeuvres Complètes* ed. M. A. Ruff, Paris, 1968, p. 43.

sense of alienation from the book. It is all a charade; he cannot really see *me*. And that, of course, is part of the consciously frigid joke which Sterne delights to pursue. He leaves a page blank for the reader to paint his picture of the widow Wadman. Has anyone ever done that? It would be a grossly literal reader who did. I remember that I in fact very nearly did, out of some obscure desire to retort the joke back upon Sterne (but then I, as this book shows, am an ill-conditioned and rebellious reader). On the other hand when Descartes in the first part of his *Discourse on Method*[61] asks the reader to have the heart of a large animal cut up in front of him, as a preparation for the anatomical argument which follows, many of his seventeenth-century readers may have sent to the shambles at once for the required article. Certainly to do so would imply no vulgar misreading, for Descartes' use of pronouns is not complicated by art.

Sterne delighted in the real absence of his reader, because it made the intimate relation he so expertly created into a particularly piquant joke. Herbert, on the other hand, escapes all this, simply because he does not address the reader at all. Or does he escape?

The answer is that he does not, but on the contrary proves vulnerable to the same attack in another and more dangerous quarter. Sterne's 'you' addressed to the reader is infected with duplicity; it is 'you' and it is also 'pseudo-you'. Herbert's 'thou' addressed to God is infected with the same duplicity, but Herbert, unlike Sterne, cannot welcome it. Devotional poetry is, after all, no place for comic illusionism.

Sterne is sometimes hailed as a sort of practitioner of stream of consciousness writing. Usually, nowadays, the comparison is at once followed by a few brisk distinctions. A distinction which is important here may be put as follows: the streams of consciousness in Virginia Woolf are usually in the form of monologue; they are conceived as the private utterance of a series of dramatic characters. The novelist magically ventilates the private mind and sensibility of first one character and then another. There is never any pretence that she is transcribing her

---

[61] In *The Philosophical Works of Descartes*, trans. E. S. Haldane and G. R. T. Ross, vol. I, Cambridge, 1911, p. 110.

own consciousness. But in Sterne there is only one consciousness, and it is ostensibly the author's. He never writes in the form of monologue. Instead, he chooses, as we have seen, pseudo-dialogue with the reader. Similarly, Herbert chooses, not the monologue-prayer form of Donne, in whose poetry as in life God rarely if ever answers, but a kind of pseudo-dialogue. Herbert, like Sterne, weaves an expert web of apparent intimacy. It was a kind of impatience with such false intimacy which provoked the question with which this book opens. When Herbert writes:

> But thou shalt answer, Lord, for me
>
> (*The Quip*)

does God, as he actually listens, start and begin to answer? No, no more than we, as readers begin to colour in the blank page in *Tristram Shandy*. Thus far the argument works powerfully for the formalists: the poems of Herbert must in that case be rhetorical and not actual prayers. But to say this is to ignore the crushing difference – so great that the two artists can hardly be held still before the mind at the same time – between Sterne and Herbert. For while Sterne laughs and capers, Herbert frets and beats against the rhetorical bars of his prison. Herbert was an Anglican Puritan.

Thus the God-directed 'thou' of Herbert's poetry is subject to more than one kind of subversion: there is the natural psychological subversion whereby 'you' can only too easily take on the meaning 'you, as I would have you be' (compare here the Mary Poppins use of 'we') – then there is the subversion worked by fictive art: 'thou' (though God himself be the object) is in the poem a fictitious character, framed by Herbert; and then there is the fundamental subversion implied by Protestant theology: as the 'I' which trusts, in so far as it is good to trust, is not the poet's but God's –

> Nay, ev'n to trust in him was also his
>
> (*The Holdfast*)

– so the 'thou' must by this reasoning become God's 'I' and the poet's 'he', a state of affairs which all but the strongest spiritual intelligences will experience as pure confusion; most certainly it paralyses both poetry and prayer. It is easy to see why pronouns engage so much of Herbert's energy:

> O be mine still! still make me thine!
> Or rather make no Thine and Mine.
>
> (*Clasping of Hands*)

But where there is no thine or mine, there can be no poetry and no prayer.

Now we must turn back for the last time, to *The Dedication*, and concentrate now on the last two lines:

> Turn their eyes hither, who shall make a gain:
> Theirs, who shall hurt themselves or me, refrain.

Herbert in this Dedication has striven to eliminate himself; it is a giving, and yet what is given is already God's and so it is no giving; yet Herbert cannot bear to be excluded and so proposes to vie with the God-made poetry in singing God's praise: 'And make us strive, who shall sing best thy name.'

The logical tension is indeed extreme. Herbert is giving God what is God's. It would be a critical error to read this as a mere trope (like 'Take all my loves, my love, yea take them all;/What has thou now more than thou hadst before?')[62] Shakespeare's lines wittily equivocate on the subjective and objective senses of 'my'. The equivocation permits – indeed it presupposes – the possibility that the lover really has his own love to give. In *The Dedication* the subjective 'my' proves to be an actual *illusion*, so that we are confronted, not so much with a tension, as with a *vanishing* paradox. It is thoroughly and finally resolved before our very eyes. Herbert really has nothing to give. Yet somehow he cannot let his paradox die, and allows the pathetic self-assertion to survive in the published poem.

The last lines remind us that these poems are to be published, that they are in a manner for our eyes. The whole poem is therefore a tense pattern of successive intrusions: God intrudes on Herbert's own address to God, Herbert competitively intrudes on that, and then we intrude on both, and thus the perfect circle of Calvinist theology ('What's good is God's') is

---

[62] Shakespeare, Sonnet XL.

subjected to a recurrent pressure from a merely human plane.

I have argued that the pronoun, inherently one of the more fluid features of language, becomes in Herbert the subject of a further crisis of confidence. Since the time of Gottlob Frege it has been customary to draw a brisk and easy distinction between sense and reference; the sense of a word is comprised in the dictionary definition, the reference is the actual thing, in the real world, to which we apply the word on any particular occasion.

'Morning star' and 'Evening star' have, as a matter of mere fact, the same reference. But, of course, sense and reference are not wholly independent of one another. The sense of a word is commonly determined or modified by habitual reference. Take the French pronoun, *vous*. One is tempted to say that the sense of *vous* is plural while its reference is often a single person. Perhaps there was a stage in the development of the French language when this simple opposition would have served. Today such simplicity is spurious. *Vous* has been applied so often and so consistently to single persons that 'polite singular address' is now one of its *lexical* functions, and provides one of the *senses* of the word. Meanwhile, the historical fact that the ordinary sense was once always plural can still be felt in the implication of courtesy and is enforced by the continued existence of *vous* as the usual plural form. But all such extensions of pronominal usage presuppose a certain stability in our conception of the objects of reference. Let us suppose that I address you as *vous* (polite form). If it were not clear to both of us that you are a single person, politeness could not be inferred. As always, significant divagation presupposes a contrasting norm. We really must know the difference, in objective fact, between one person and many, between the self and others. But in Herbert it is just this objective certainty which is exposed to doubt. In *The Temple* the presumed reference of 'I' in such expressions as 'I trust thee' may be not the self but God. Thus the stable groundwork of identity by which alone the excesses of an inherently mutinous linguistic form are to be controlled, is finally removed. Herbert's theology implies that ordinary language is unusable. Yet he has succeeded, by words alone, in telling us just that.

# THE REFLEXIVE CHECK

I HAVE tried to show that Herbert's poetry owes much of its life to a kind of death-wish. Incorrigibly it invites the destructive question, 'But what about your own activity in all this?' Questions of this kind work by transposing the logical order of discourse. Such lateral moves in argument have a long history in philosophy. 'There is nothing in the mind which was not in the senses first', says the empiricist. 'Unless the mind itself', answers the lateral critic. 'All meaningful sentences are either analytic or else founded on the senses', says the logical positivist; 'The statement you just made is neither', comes the answer. Perhaps the purest example is Grelling's 'heterological paradox': all words are either instances of themselves (in which case they are 'homological') or else not (in which case they are 'heterological'); 'English' is homological because 'English' is English, but 'French' is heterological; 'français', on the other hand, is homological; 'word' is homological; 'polysyllabic' is homological but 'monosyllabic' is heterological. What then of 'heterological' itself? Is it heterological or homological? The paralysing answer is then given: if it is heterological it must be homological and if it is homological it must be heterological. This and associated paradoxes moved Bertrand Russell to formulate his theory of logical types, precisely in order to provide an escape from such contradictions by breaking the closed circle of a one-plane logic. But, as often as not, this mode of criticism expresses itself in a well-placed adverb: 'Plato banishes the poet from his commonwealth, but he does so very poetically. . . .'

In the present study I have availed myself of this mode of criticism many times. It is now necessary to consider its credentials. If the method itself is to become the object of discussion we need a short way of referring to it. If verbal coinage were more in fashion and the world kinder, I would offer the word 'nisi-ipseity', formed, with a learned barbarism greater even than that of the mediaeval *haecceity* ('this-ness'), from the paradigm phrase already cited: 'Nihil in intellectu quod non prius in sensu, *nisi ipse* intellectus', 'Nothing in the mind which was not first in the senses, *unless* the mind *itself*'. 'Nisi-ipseity' has the merit of referring the hearer to the essential locution of such criticism, which is 'Unless the x itself is . . .'. But the word is unacceptable and I shall therefore not so much as mention it in this book (this small *occupatio* is offered, to those readers who might wish to apply this mode of criticism to me, as a limbering-up exercise).

An alternative phrase, slightly more digestible perhaps, is 'ontological check', where 'ontological' refers to the different levels of being proposed by a Christian culture: thus at one ontological level (that of fiction) Falstaff laughs with Hal, at another Shakespeare laughs with both and, at a third, God — God does whatever God would do. But the word has certain metaphysical implications which one might not wish to endorse; in particular, the notion of orders of *being* is suspect; Hamlet does not '*be*' in any distinctive manner; he is merely a different sort of thing from Shakespeare; he is a fiction. Thus a less portentous word is needed. The best I can do (and as it does not explain itself the reader is asked to remember it as a technical term) is 'reflexive check'.

In *The Dedication* the reflexive check can be applied twice. First we apply it by imagining that God is actually reading the poem addressed to him as it is written. This produces a certain indignation at the presence in the lines of residual, unremoved, unregenerate human wit. Second, we may imagine the reader watching while Herbert prays. In both cases we have a sense that we are breaking some *taboo* or rule, and that is because we are allowing, first, God himself, the real God and, second, the real reader to intrude in the fictional space of the poem. But Herbert can scarcely complain since he has, so to speak, invited them in. Herbert's poetry, unlike Homer's, keeps open house and the result is extremely trying on the nerves.

This intrusion of reality is in some ways analogous to the intrusion of reality in Anselm's ontological proof of the existence of God in the second chapter of his *Proslogion*. Anselm argued that, if God is defined as that which is better than we can conceive, he must exist; an island which really exists is obviously better than a merely notional island; but if God did not exist we could immediately suppose him made better, by mentally ascribing real existence to him; but *ex hypothesi* he is better than we can imagine and so must already possess all the merits which we might attribute to him; so he must already have existence; therefore he exists. The effect is of a metaphysical conjuring trick. We seemed to be discussing the *definition* or the *concept* of God when suddenly we were, so to speak, struck down from behind by his actual existence.

Of course, we are free to resist the ontological intrusion in Anselm's proof: we may say, 'Existence is not a predicate!' or 'All it shows is that if God did exist he would *have to* exist'. But Herbert cannot resist in this way. The intrusion of God into a poem can never be rejected by a good Protestant, since in truth there is no pious art in which he does not already exert his creative power. Indeed it is not so much a matter of permitting the divine intrusion as of confessing the divine presence. Herbert's *Dedication* begins by recognizing all of this; but then it *frets*, and in that discontented fidgeting the poetry can live and reach us, the readers.

We can now turn to those poems which most audaciously — that is, with the greatest death-wish — lay themselves open to a reflexive check: *The Storm*, *Love III*, *Artillerie* and *The Holdfast*.

### The Storm

If as the windes and waters here below
    Do flie and flow,
My sighs and tears as busie were above;
    Sure they would move
And much affect thee, as tempestuous times
Amaze poore mortals, and object their crimes.

Starres have their storms, ev'n in a high degree,
    As well as we.
A throbbing conscience spurred by remorse
    Hath a strange force:
It quits the earth, and mounting more and more
Dares to assault thee, and beseige thy doore.

> There it stands knocking, to thy musicks wrong,
>   And drowns the song.
> Glorie and honour are set by, till it
>   An answer get.
> Poets have wrong'd poore storms: such dayes are best;
> They purge the aire without, within the breast.

Implicit in this poem is the sense that one cannot hope to move the Omniscient by argument. Yet at the same time it seems to find an opening for suasive prayer. For if we merely sigh and weep in an innocent passion of grief, it may be (to avail ourselves of the proleptic causality of Calvinism) that God *will have been* moved by our uncalculating simplicity. Here Herbert, within the scheme of his poem, presents himself as a discordant intruder on the harmony of Heaven, an innocently importunate child (the idea has occurred to us before). Moreover, as children do who come downstairs after bed-time, he hopes to prevail by his very artlessness. But — now we apply the reflexive check — what of the poet who has become fully conscious of the efficacy of tears? Has he not forfeited his innocence? Can he ever weep again without a consciousness of interest? In the moral background of this poem there lurks the repellent and ultimately self-refuting idea of artificially inducing emotions *because* emotions are non-artificial and may therefore turn out to have influenced God. The reasoning may seem strained but there can be little doubt that Puritans 'jacked up' their emotions in exactly this way.

The reader may object that my contrast between art and simplicity is imposed on the poem and appears nowhere in it. To me it is implicit in every line. But for such unsympathetic readers I need an equivalent example, if possible not theological. I offer *Love III*, in so far as that poem deals with a certain paradox involved in the concept of humility.

> Love bade me welcome: yet my soul drew back,
>   Guiltie of dust and sinne.
> But quick-ey'd Love, observing me grow slack
>   From my first entrance in,
> Drew nearer to me, sweetly questioning,
>   If I lack'd any thing.

A guest, I answer'd, worthy to be here:
    Love said, You shall be he.
I the unkinde, ungratefull? Ah my deare,
    I cannot look on thee,
Love took my hand, and smiling did reply,
    Who made the eyes but I?

Truth Lord, but I have marr'd them: let my shame
    Go where it doth deserve.
And know you not, sayes Love, who bore the blame?
    My deare, then I will serve.
You must sit down, sayes Love, and taste my meat:
    So did I sit and eat.

Here once more we have a situation in which a very small quantum of reflexive intelligence can cost you your innocence. Is 'I am humble' a self-refuting sentence? If the speaker is unaware that humility is a virtue, it need not be. But Christians are so *instructed*, and in this way the paradox is generated. The difficulty can of course be more or less skilfully disguised, and some writers really do seem to be protected by a sort of unconsciousness. For example, the fourteenth-century mystic and lunatic Marjorie Kempe, who in her *Book* remorselessly disparages herself as 'this creature' even as she recounts her holy exploits, seems genuinely unaware of the effect (considerably beyond that produced by Uriah Heep) her language will have on a sophisticated ear. In practice such a reader is obliged to grow more sophisticated still and to correct his response in deference to her simplicity. In a very different work such as Sir Thomas Browne's *Religio Medici* I take the effect to be rather one of mannered dissimulation. Browne is for ever ruefully acknowledging that he cannot match the hatred and intolerance of his coaevals and all is well as long as our attention is fixed on the public evil of intolerance. But the repeated 'I' of the autobiographical mode must in the end assert its presence and so we begin to ask, 'Why must the example of tolerance always be Browne himself?'

In *Love III* Herbert seeks to deal with the problem not by suppressing the intelligence but by stretching it. He first acknowledges and then seeks to transcend the paradox. For a while there is an impression in the poem of that moral competition with God which we found elsewhere, the attempt to out-do God himself in self-abnegation, to reject the divine beneficence not from hatred but from sheer altruism and self-contempt. But this, as Herbert well knows, is only a form of pride. Thus, in this poem, the paradox whereby 'I am humble' is self-refuting is squarely faced and gently set aside. To be sure, the speaker in the poem has not reached the pitch of congratulating himself on his own humility, but the danger of this is perhaps not wholly absent from the moral penumbra of the poem. As it stands, we perceive that the speaker's humility, in so far as it is still self-regarding, is not yet deep enough. To say 'I am not worthy' is presumptuous in so far as it implies that desert is any way relevant to the case. God's answer must be a smiling, 'Whatever made you think these things were done according to *desert*?' What is rather needed, then, is the *utter* humility which acknowledges the sheer irrelevance of personal merit. And this humility, now defined as the true sort, is by definition non-self-regarding and therefore exempt from the self-consumption we noted earlier. Thus Herbert in the moral structure of his poem transcends the problem of an asserted humility. The humility asserted is engulfed in a larger humility which makes no claim at all.

So is the problem solved? I answer, not at all. A man who can explain with intricate accuracy the detailed structure of his respiratory system cannot cease to breathe, since air is the medium in which he lives. George Herbert as the man who prays within the poem may be corrected 'from outside', but the lines 'from outside' were provided by (once more) George Herbert. The George Herbert who lives inside the poem, *Love III*, may be unconscious that he has found real humility, but what of the George Herbert who artfully made the whole poem? Such innocence will henceforth be all but unattainable for *him*. We may think for a moment of poor T. S. Eliot, who had the ill luck to be assured by St John of the Cross that when God seemed furthest off he was really very near; thus it is when we feel most abandoned that we have real cause for hope. Thereafter Eliot could, naturally, never attain the requisite anguish of spirit. In *Four Quartets* the Dark Night of the Soul remains only a bookish myth; the poem moves, as it were, in a northern summer night, where it never really gets dark. Here to be sure lay an opportunity for a *further* despair ('for some/Not to be martyrs is a martyrdom') and so by implication for a secondary operation of grace from God. But one can grow tired of following through these cycles of the spirit, which can be indefinitely prolonged.

In *Love III* the reflexive check was applied by Herbert as poet before we as critics applied it to him. When he implicitly accused his fictional self of displayiing pride in the very act of disclaiming it, he showed us the way. What Herbert the poet did to Herbert the character we in turn can do to Herbert the poet. Thus we may find an insinuation of virtue in his repudiation of the very notion of desert.

In *Artillerie* a star from Heaven falls as a spark into Herbert's lap and (very naturally) he hastily brushes it away. Whereupon God (if not naturally, then typically) rebukes him:

> *Do as thou usest, disobey,*
> *Expell good motions from thy breast,*
> *Which have the face of fire, but end in rest*

which is as much as to say 'As usual, I give you a good thing and you throw it away.'

It might be objected that my coarse paraphrase capitalizes on what is really no more than a momentary crossing of lines, a temporary confusion of tenor and vehicle. It is reasonable to brush away a spark, but it is not so reasonable to reject a motion from God, and *that* is what the poem is really about. Nevertheless, a sense persists that the momentary discomfort is somehow revealing, is part of a larger pattern of disquiet. The confusion of tenor and vehicle is rigged for God's advantage; Herbert recoils from a spark and is blamed for recoiling from God. This incongruity reflects the systematically defeated nature of Puritan devotion, in which every impulse of the praying subject is somehow anticipated and rendered irrelevant by God. Moreoever, just as in *Redemption*, Christ granted the suit before it was put to him, so here Herbert is rebuked for disobedience before he has knowingly disobeyed. Thus the shift from tenor to vehicle is not so much an oversight as an extremely subtle allusion to the proleptic causality of Calvinism.

Herbert within the poem responds with a dignified acceptance of the rebuke and a professed willingness to suffer whatever is in consequence required (he does not say, 'But I thought it was a spark'!). But then he begins to fight back, pointing out that he has sent *his* communications to Heaven, and then, with something of the extraordinary gall we found in *Afflication IV*, reminds his maker that although God's personal obligation to Herbert is infinitely less than Herbert's to God, the deity is nevertheless bound by his own promise to answer prayers. But then the poem ends (as *Affliction IV* does not end) by voicing exactly the disquiet I have just expressed:

There is no articling with thee.

Within the poem the reflexive check applies to Herbert's attempt to negotiate; his very negotiation is in fact a continuation of the headstrong opposition he seeks to disclaim. Outside the poem we sense, by a parallel reflexive check, that the disclaiming of power to negotiate is itself offered as a kind of pious work. Calvinism is cruel enough even for this. Poor Herbert cannot help trying to deserve God's love. He is like that sort of lover who does not know when to stop apologizing.

To those who say that such an interpretation is strained the answer is simple. I grant that most Anglican readers never draw the conclusions I have drawn. But they have inferred that Herbert is a kind of saint, and that (if we remember Luther's remark that a 'holy man' is a contradiction in terms) is enough. Herbert has only to be as perceptive about his poems as the ordinary reader to realize that he has insinuated his merit yet again. The stricter sort of Puritan, who outlawed all devotional poetry and stuck to psalms, would have seen it at once. Indeed it is likely that Herbert himself would be the first to admit the appropriateness of this critique. So far is it from being an anachronistic reading that we can say with confidence, all the time *he knew*. Alone of Herbert's critics Stanley Fish gets it right: 'Every moral stance entails a presumption that must be disavowed, and every disavowal immediately re-establishes the presumption.'[63]

[63] *Self-consuming Artifacts*, p. 182.

But the most intensely reflexive of all the poems, and the one which at the same time comes nearest to breaking the infinite regress, is *The Holdfast*.

> I threatned to observe the strict decree
>> Of my deare God with all my power & might.
> But I was told by one, it could not be;
> Yet I might trust in God to be my light.
> Then will I trust, said I, in him alone.
>> Nay, ev'n to trust in him, was also his:
> We must confesse that nothing is our own.
> Then I confesse that he my succour is:
> But to have nought is ours, not to confesse
>> That we have nought. I stood amaz'd at this,
>> Much troubled, till I heard a friend expresse,
> That all things were more ours by being his.
>> What Adam had, and forfeited for all,
>> Christ keepeth now, who cannot fail or fall.

We should have learned by now not to be surprised that the cataclysmic ending of this poem, in which the demons of Calvin are driven back, should be expressed, not in glittering imagery, but in a kind of mute war of *pronouns*. The words which set George Herbert's world upright again are in themselves colourless: 'more ours by being his'. We drink the words thirstily because they are so exactly what we need. Moral autonomy is given back to man, and reconciled with piety.

But cold reflection gradually revives and begins to fret at the proffered resolution. What does Herbert mean by this shining mystical equivox, both 'ours' and 'his'? Somehow this is not like the great traditional paradoxes of Christianity. 'Whose service is perfect freedom' is profoundly rational, for it is perfectly true that by accepting the law of obligation we enter the great kingdom of moral action, otherwise closed to us. Likewise Hopkins' 'All mine, yet common to my every peer' is, at a lower level, both credible and just, since the beauty of the world is indeed at one's disposal and yet one's enjoyment of it is of the kind which deprives no one. But the doubts aroused by Herbert's paradox are less easily allayed. What if the line serves merely to express the need to evoke the mere outward shape of the wished-for answer, and really offers no substantial resolution at all?

In fact the only solid meaning which the poem can give to 'ours' is 'not in danger of being lost'. Imagine a child who is in the habit of losing his weekly fifty-pence piece. He therefore gives it to his father for safe-keeping. We might say that the fifty-pence piece is 'more safely his' than it was before; I do not think we should say that it is 'more his'. Yet Herbert can find no better support for his assertion of man's moral powers. And when we consider the need this formula is designed to satisfy its inadequacy is only too obvious. Herbert had wished to be autonomously and reciprocally good, in *return* for the goodness of God. It is as if the child in our analogy were to say to his father, 'Never mind these fifty-pence pieces I keep losing; what I would really like is to do a paper-round, so that I could earn some money myself and give *you* fifty pence for once; then it would really be *my* fifty pence I'd be giving, not just pocket money from you', and the father were then to reply, 'If you want it to be really *your* money, just give me the fifty pence I gave you on Friday and I'll keep it safe, and then it will really remain your property instead of getting lost'. Quite clearly, in this conversation the father has completely missed the point. Yet the latent logic of Herbert's poem is in no better case. Herbert piously blurs his own reasoning to make God seem better. Nevertheless, let us give due honour to *The Holdfast*, which, if it did not overthrow Calvin, at least resisted him.

Elsewhere the Calvinist pattern is distressingly perfect. Again and again the harsh denial of human merit is eagerly embraced by the poet as affording an opportunity for further humiliation. Again and again the poems turn and abuse poetry itself, by which alone they live. God's dictation may successfully terminate a poem but it can never constitute a poem. *The Dedication* of *The Temple* is by Herbert (let us not cavil) and is a poem. The epigraph to *The Church*, which reads quite simply,

> *Glory be to* God *on high*
> *And on earth peace*
> *Good will towards men*

was dictated by angels to the shepherds and is beyond poetry. If man's separate essence consists in his sinfulness, if *esse est peccare*, then, equally, Herbert's poetry consists of sentences successively condemned in the poems, but happily never actually erased. The poems show inadequate conceptions cancelled one after another, but without all this despised and cancelled matter there would be no poems. Not only does Herbert allow the offending lines to stand, he even, as in *Jordan I* and *II*, passes twice over the river of valediction, thus making it doubly clear that the things he is rejecting have a hold on his heart no less tenacious than that of the Promised Land itself. Though *Deus obstat*, the human poetry is quietly given its *imprimatur*.

In *The Temper I* Herbert, as often, projects upon God a confessedly futile suasive argument; he tells God that, though from the divine point of view Herbert's torments are very small, from the human point of view they are overwhelming. Here the theology is frankly bad and indeed is oddly like that solemnly advanced by Pope in *An Essay on Man*, where it is explained that one can hardly expect a cosmic tycoon like God to suspend his heavenly wheeling (and dealing) and the implied Newtonian laws just because an avalanche happens to be falling on blameless Bethell.[64] In Pope even the words in Matthew's Gospel about the fall of a sparrow are used to convey not divine concern but divine equanimity:

> Who sees with equal eye, as God of all,
> A hero perish, or a sparrow fall.[65]

Herbert, to be sure, knows better than this, but he allows the lines to stand:

> O rack me not to such a vast extent;
>   Those distances belong to thee
>   The world's too little for thy tent
> A grave too big for me.

It is as if, while formally addressing God, he is muttering sentiments under his breath for us, his friends, to hear, senti-

---

[64] *An Essay on Man*, IV, 126–8.
[65] ibid., I. 87–8.

ments which he knows could not stand up in court: 'Yes, officer, but you may not have noticed that the sun was in my eyes and (*sotto voce*) you're an officious clown, that's what you are!' But then the thunderous Protestant doctrine supervenes.

The subtlest example of this art of making poems from the residuum left by theology is *The Pulley*:

When God at first made man,
  Having a glasse of blessings standing by;
Let us (said he) poure on him all we can:
Let the worlds riches, which dispersed lie,
  Contract into a span.

So strength first made a way;
  Then beautie flow'd, then wisdome, honour, pleasure:
When almost all was out, God made a stay,
Perceiving that alone of all his treasure
  Rest in the bottome lay.

For if I should (said he)
  Bestow this jewell also on my creature,
He would adore my gifts in stead of me,
And rest in Nature, not the God of Nature:
  So both should losers be.

Yet let him keep the rest,
  But keep them with repining restlessnesse:
Let him be rich and wearie, that at least,
If goodnesse leade him not, yet wearinesse
  May tosse him to my breast.

The last stanza, with its almost voluptuous combining of lassitude and exaltation (the word 'tosse' is perfectly in place, surprising and yet appropriate) employs a paradox. God would have man possess good things and yet at the same time be discontented with them, so that even if he does not reach God by goodness (for example, by love of God or gratitude for his bounty) sheer boredom will send him thither by default. This, if taken with solemn literalness, would mean that there are two ways of getting to God; one is by goodness and the other is by discontent with earthly things, that is, 'divine discontent'. This last in another context might have looked just like piety or virtue. Herbert has exaggerated the contrast with gratitude to a point where he can call one good and the other not good, entirely in order to generate a purely *literary* paradox. A certain sort of theologically minded critic might try to get rid of this spurious ethical contrast with some such paraphrase as: 'If love of bounty lead him not to me, then discontent with all that is *not* me may likewise bring him home.' But that is not what Herbert wrote.

Helen Vendler, who has written admirably on this poem, notices how Herbert deigns to employ a humanizing myth according to which God can change his mind and draws attention to 'an edge or frame of frivolity'. She adds,

> We end by suspecting that for poetic purposes at least an arrangement of existence which can yield the complexities of the last stanza of *The Pulley* is preferable to one in which everything should have been absolute.[66]

But it would be idle to pretend that all of Herbert's poetry consists of theologically rejected matter. The rejections, the transcendings, even the divine answers when joined to the rest clearly help to make poetry. Otherwise, Herbert would really be the player poet I have laboured to rule out. In *The Pulley* itself, part of the *literary* impact, the poem's power to move us, lies in the fact that we know the opposition between goodness and weariness to be provisional and factitious, a paper screen to shield our eyes from a brightness too strong for ordinary sight. And this is religion. Of course we may still say that Herbert likes to show not just the splendour which transcends but also the human folly which is so transcended. But then piety may delight both in truth and in the emergence of truth.

Nevertheless, there remain those poems in which there is far more unregenerate matter than regenerate and here a different answer is required. One with which I have flirted in these last pages is that the impulse to include such material must be purely literary; here at least is a *part* of Herbert which suits the

[66] *The Poetry of George Herbert*, p. 37.

games-playing theory of poetry. But still something is wrong. And indeed it is the most important thing of all.

It is as if, in blind historicist deference to Calvin, we had forgotten the real content of this theologically condemned material. It is, of course, from beginning to end, love of God. If *esse est peccare* let us not forget that in Herbert *peccare est amare*. Here Calvin had his death-wound, though Herbert never knew what he had done.

## VII

## THE LESSONS OF *THE TEMPLE*

Popular religions are really, in the conception of their more vulgar votaries, a species of daemonism; and the higher the deity is exalted in power and knowledge, the lower of course is he depressed in goodness and benevolence; whatever epithets of praise may be bestowed on him by his amazed adorers. Among idolaters, the words may be false, and belie the secret opinion: But among more exalted religionists, the opinion itself contracts a kind of falsehood, and belies the inward sentiment. The heart secretly detests such measures of cruel and implacable vengeance; but the judgement dares not but pronounce them perfect and adorable. And the additional misery of this inward struggle aggravates all the other terrors by which these unhappy victims to superstition are for ever hunted.[67]

* *

I HAVE found Herbert's poetry to be riven by moral and theological contradiction. I have further argued that this frequency of contradiction implies not that Herbert's poetry is theologically superficial but the reverse. The repeated ἀπορίαι, the intellectual impasses of Herbert's poetry at last compose a fundamental if largely unconscious critique of Calvinism. Herbert's poetry pierces the contemporary theology of Protestantism to the half-Platonic Augustinian ontology which lies behind it.

The underlying notions are, first, that every degree of creation is a degree of evil and, second, that every degree of evil is a

[67] David Hume, *The Natural History of Religion*, in *Essays, Moral, Political and Literary*, ed. T. H. Green and T. H. Grose, 1875, vol. II, pp. 354–5.

degree of un-being. As they stand the phrases are almost unintelligible. We may climb back to them by way of the more familiar doctrines of Calvin. Calvin's mind (in this he resembles the Gnostics and the Manichaeans) was binary; for him things are either all good or all bad. Anything all-good is God. Thus the created universe, in so far as it is distinct from God, is bad. And, of course, creation implies distinction. The redisposition of the infinite divine essence could hardly count as *making*. Thus creation directly implies evil in so far as it implies the coexistence of God and not God. Here we may see a harshly exaggerated version of one very old solution to the Problem of Evil: *non essent omnia, aequalia si essent*, 'All things would never have been, had all things been equal';[68] that is, if all things had been equally good, all things would have been perfect and so indistinguishable from God, in which case they could not be said to have been created at all as separate existents. The answer to the Problem of Evil is thus (quite powerfully) *ad hominem*: 'In complaining that God permits evil to exist, you are complaining that he has permitted *you* to exist. Do you really want to do that?' Accordingly, for Calvin God makes a black universe and could *make* nothing else. This is the blank transcendence of Calvinism whereby the universe is not full of God but is rather by its very essence the absence of God. There is in traditional Christianity a word for this absence. It is 'Hell'.

It may be objected that if Calvin's God is transcendent he is also ubiquitously immanent, since he is present in every authentically virtuous act, every movement of mathematical competence, every discovery of natural science. But God is not so much 'present in' these things as constitutive of them. He proleptically usurps all goodness, and always in Calvin there is a sense that the created universe is set aside or crushed in such usurpation (though 'usurpation' is really the wrong word, since this territory was always his). Such 'immanence' serves only to humiliate, to emphasize the real depravity of *created* man. The two Augustinian theses with which we began,

---

[68] Augustine, *De Diversis Quaestionibus LXXXIII*, q. xli, in Migne, *Patrologia Latina*, vol. XL, p. 27.

namely that every degree of creation is a degree of evil, and every degree of evil is a degree of unbeing, are in fact contradictory. To create something is to give it being. Augustine can never forget this for long and the main weight of his theology is finally behind the proposition that in so far as any created thing exists it is good. In Calvin the opposite principle triumphed. Thus his theology is the dark obverse of Spinozistic pantheism, since all solid good is God and the rest is 'a mess of shadows'. But nothing created is Godly, or in any way good. Both Leibniz and Spinoza find it easy to think of God as essentially creative, because for them the creation blazes with God. This is because at the end of the seventeenth century theology managed somehow to rid itself of all memory of the Fall of Man. Within a few years Pope, consciously echoing Milton with his 'vindicate the ways of God to man',[69] succeeded in conducting the entire vindication without a single reference to Adam's sin. With Calvin it is otherwise. The predestinate fall of Adam determines all that follows. Thus in Calvinist theology the very fact of creation constitutes a problem: if creation can only mean the introduction of evil, if God's goodness was infinite before, why create at all?

This Calvin cannot really solve, but the answer he offers is at least 'in character'. God creates the great darkness of nature as an arena for his own spectacular exertion of redemptive good; redemption is God's reassimilation to himself of that which he had originally invested in the creation of man. The basely mercenary meaning originally implied in the metaphor 're-deem', made by the poetry of Herbert to seem movingly incongruous with the real love of God, is in Calvin merely appropriate. Faced with this problem, the mind may be driven to play desperate tricks with the very concepts of being and non-being, creator and creation. If Jehovah, Yah-weh, 'I am who am', is the being whose essence is existence, then perhaps that which is not God is at root a kind of non-being, a mere negation. For Augustine (in opposition to the Manichaeans) evil is so construed. In this case, in permitting a depraved world God is guilty of no solid action, since the depraved world is only a

[69] *An Essay on Man*, I. 16.

mode of un-being. It is, if you like, not so much a piece of constructive creation as a mere logical implication of God's existence; God implies not-God, and we are the not-God he implies. This tormented reasoning can at last be made to yield the conclusion (only to be used on certain special occasions), 'evil does not exist'. Further conclusions, such as 'Adam did not fall' and 'The universe was never created', are not encouraged. The other possible conclusion is of course a merry antinomianism, and this actually happened, though not with official approval.

There are thus two stages to Calvinism. God does the good but man ('responsibly'!) does the evil. But man's evil nature was given to him by God. So (it might reasonably be concluded) God really does the evil too. Calvin, to be sure, avails himself of the Boethian stratagem whereby Adam fell freely though God foreknew that he would fall.[70] But by the more radical philosophy, evil is inherent in the fact of creation and that, certainly, is the work of God. Calvin consistently opposed the moderate view of Melanchthon that God 'permitted' sin, and instead affirmed with Zwingli that sin happens by God's will.[71] We are thus confronted with the dual character of God's agency; as creator he works evil, as self-lover, good. It is this implicit horror which George Herbert's poetry exposes and refutes.

For Herbert's poetry begins by claiming a kind of merit for the creature, for the depraved not-God, and so makes the first breach in Calvin's uncompromising scheme. Then, by the very generosity of its submission to God, it begins to suggest (contrary to its own professed intention) that virtue is not *residually* present in man but is rather *uniquely* present, that virtue exists in man and in man alone. We are admitted to a world in which the darkness can love the light while the light can only love itself. Certainly Herbert would not have it so and, when in *The Thanksgiving* he alludes to the unmatchable Passion of Christ, he effectively presents God as authentically generous. But he can do so only by forgetting his Calvinism. Both Passion and

[70] *Institutes*, I. xv. 8 and II. ii. *passim*.
[71] See A. M. Hunter, *The Teaching of Calvin*, Glasgow, 1920, p. 137.

Redemption in Calvin's scheme proceed from the purest self-love.

Moreover, Herbert subjects the thesis, 'All the good we do is really done by God' to a scrutiny which ultimately, against his intention, destroys it. 'Nous n'avons ni pensees ni affections, comme j'ay dit, qui ne soyent rebelles à la justice de Dieu', writes Calvin.[72] It is a proposition to which he loves to return in the Sermons: 'Quand nous entrons en ce monde, desia nous sommes ennemis de Dieu, il n'y a que malice et rebellion en nous ... il n'y a pas une seule goutte de bien.'[73] 'Nous ne pouvons pas avoir une seule bonne pensée. Qu est-ce que l'homme en soy? Un ennemi mortel de Dieu, et de tout bien.'[74] Calvin is clear that we are the enemies of God in every affection of our hearts. 'Including', the poetry of Herbert obstinately asks, 'the love of God?' Whichever answer Calvin gives destroys him. If he says 'No, not the love of God', his doctrine of total depravity is in ruins. If he says, 'It is not you who love God, but God working in you', he empties that love of all generosity, all virtue. The love of the creature reaching out of darkness is one thing, the love of the all-powerful for himself is another. If one is to be meritorious and the other not, which would we naturally choose? Not as Calvin teaches. What Herbert's poetry does is to fasten on those aspects of the moral life which are *essentially* creaturely, which simply make no sense if transferred to the Creator, namely resignation, surrender, trust, faith, submission. To give these to God is not to reform ethics but to destroy it.

Thus Calvin's picture of God in the world, already sufficiently grim, is shown to be even darker than we thought. It had seemed that, even if God created man for total depravity and predestined him to damnation, at least he also wrought those impulses of good which can still be found in us. But Herbert's poetry shows that this very work of God, once it is seen to be his, ceases to be good, at least in so far as it applies to the deepest acts of worship.

[72] Sermon XLI, on Deuteronomy 5; in *Opera*, vol. XXVI, 1883, p. 378.
[73] Sermon LII, on Job xiv, ibid., vol. XXXIII, p. 657.
[74] Sermon LXXXVIII, on Job xxiii, ibid., vol. XXXIV, p. 334. c.f. Sermon CLIII, on Deuteronomy, xxviii, ibid., vol. XXVIII, p. 347.

At this point it is only fair that I should apply to myself the test I have applied to others. Suppose Herbert were to read, over my shoulder, the words I have just written. What would his reaction be? Of course he would fight like a tiger against every word. But he would be forced in the end to cut off his Calvinism to save his religion.

# VIII

## INNOCENCE AND EXPERIENCE

WHAT THEN, of the insight with which we began, namely, that Herbert's *manipulation* of his own humiliation and God's triumph, once noticed, nullifies the proffered humility? We have had much to say about 'the loss of innocence' which occurs when a humble man realizes that his humility counts as a virtue. The notion appears to be relevant here. For, if Herbert knew that he had triumphed in the deep, underlying theological competition with God, if he knew that he had finally demonstrated that only man could be generous, once more the entire enterprise would collapse in cynicism. Once again, the knowledge that he had won would mean that after all he had not; that sweet submission with which the human subject transcends the blank self-glorification of God would now be no more than a feigned submission. Or else, more mysteriously, the poems might stand as a dramatization, from outside, by one excluded by insight from participation, of the way a more innocent version of himself might actually triumph over Calvin's God.

It seems likely that Herbert intended neither of these things. His innocence, though shaken, is still real enough to afford him some protection. Certainly his humility begins to doubt itself, certainly he begins to shudder at the knowledge that he is playing God's part. But that God is really better than himself he never doubts. For, though the danger of *seeming* to have won in the moral struggle with God may occasionally arise, Herbert never suspected that he had really won. And, of course, as we have seen, any such suspicion would instantly have cancelled his victory. At the same time, it is likely that, in the periods of meditation and self-examination which must have preceded *The Temple*, anyone as intelligent as Herbert must have glanced nervously down many of the tortuous by-ways through which we, with a carelessness proper to this century, . have marched. But most probably at such times he would simply have judged himself confused by vain speculation, trapped by false casuistry.

We may glimpse here the reason for a phenomenon which has long puzzled historians of ideas, that is, the ill-grounded yet almost universal contempt expressed by the greatest minds of Protestant Europe in the seventeenth century for scholastic metaphysics. These men were both penetrating and scrupulous, but there were reasons why they dared not think. Thus the intellectual labours of a Boethius, an Aquinas or a Scotus become in *Paradise Lost* the futile ramblings of the inhabitants of Hell:

> Others apart sat on a hill retired
> In thoughts more elevate, and reasoned high
> Of providence, foreknowledge, will and fate,
> Fixed fate, free will, foreknowledge absolute,
> And found no end, in wandering mazes lost.
>
> (II. 557–61)

But, to be sure, Milton's inextinguishable intellect is soon drawn into the same debate (one can sense a quickening of philosophical interest in the adjectives of the fourth line quoted). In *The Temple* Herbert thought just a little too long for his own comfort; certainly too long for Calvin's.

To argue, as I have done, that Herbert's poetry overthrows Calvinism by subjecting it to the test of ingenuous loyalty will be dismissed by many people as merely 'silly-clever'. Few now believe that Milton, by pertinaciously striving (and failing) to justify the ways of God to man, ended by proving them unjust. Similarly, David Hume's remark to Boswell that it took Locke and Clarke to make a real atheist of him[75] is often treated as a

---

[75] *Private Papers of James Boswell*, ed. Geoffrey Scott and Frederick A. Pottle, vol. XII, 1931, p. 227.

mere joke. Yet the real impetus of ideas, as they disengage themselves from the local and particular intentions of their first proponents, often works in this way. Hume's own horrifyingly sceptical philosophy was crucial in producing, in the mind of Immanuel Kant (remember how *The Treatise* broke in upon his 'dogmatic slumbers') the most developed positive philosophy of the modern world. But to see this you must take your thinkers and your poets seriously. The cartographer of rhetorical convention, on the other hand, unlike Kant, may sleep secure.

# II. PARADISE LOST

---

## I

## THE FATHER TALKS TO THE SON

Only begotten Son, seest thou what rage
Transports our adversary, whom no bounds
Prescribed, no bars of hell, nor all the chains
Heaped on him there, nor yet the main abyss
Wide interrupt can hold; so bent he seems
On desperate revenge, that shall redound
Upon his own rebellious head. . . .

(*Paradise Lost*, III. 80–6)[1]

MILTON, like Herbert, writes dialogue for God. The rules of the game, however, have obviously changed. This voice is a good deal less intimate than the voice which breathed 'Child' in Herbert's ear – indeed the very thought of this Miltonic voice approaching one's ear is enough to cause an involuntary protective movement of the hand to the head. Milton does not pretend that he knows what God is saying to him. Why should he, when he knows what God is saying *to himself*? In *Lycidas* Phoebus touched the poet's trembling ears in admonition, but

---

[1] All verse quotations from Milton are from *The Poems of John Milton*, ed. John Carey and Alistair Fowler, 1968.

not as he had done to Virgil in the sixth Eclogue. There the Cynthian warned the poet against attempting an epic theme beyond his strength. In *Lycidas* the poet is advised to forget merely mortal fame since the real thing is waiting for him in heaven. As in *Lycidas*, so in *Paradise Lost*, we may say, Milton's ambition is made of sterner stuff.

I have called this speech less intimate than the divine words in Herbert. Yet surely, it might be thought, there is a sense in which it ought to have seemed far more intimate. For here the interlocutor is no mere human subject but the second person of the Trinity. The communication of God with the praying subject is a mysterious thing but it is one with which our own inward experience is conceivably involved; the dialogue of God with God (or, if we allow Milton's Arianism to be present in *Paradise Lost*) the divine Father with the divine Son, is something utterly private. Yet in Milton the communings of the Trinity sound very much like an address to a public meeting. But perhaps this is not necessarily an error on Milton's part. To essay the real inwardness of God's thought – that would have been the real mistake. To choose instead a voice slightly too large for ordinary reception, within the conventions of an epic diction, is no bad provisional solution.

Some things in this speech, however, remain hard to accept. It pleases God to be facetious at the Devil's expense and this naturally moves neither love nor adoration in the reader. Addison objected to the quibbles in Milton; the pun on 'transports' is perhaps the least forgivable in the whole poem. From joyless mirth God proceeds to philosophic apologia. There is no sign of the deeply troubling moral engagement of the subject with the Creator which we found in Herbert. Instead we have a grosser presumptuousness. Milton, having promised the justification of God's ways to man, now undertakes to present God's justification of himself. And all the time, as Milton wrote, God (we may with piety suppose) watched and listened.

The main tenor of the style at this point is rich and majestic. But there are moments when we seem to catch a shriller note:

> whose fault?
> Whose but his own? Ingrate, he had of me

All he could have; I made him just and right,
Sufficient to have stood, though free to fall.

(96–9)

Here the thought becomes urgent, with a sort of gigantesque
impetuosity (to read it is rather like watching a very big athlete
playing hop-scotch). Aristotle, Boethius, and Augustine are
woven powerfully together to form a stout fabric of common
Christianity, more Arminian than Calvinist, perhaps, but never
merely sectarian. God, no doubt, read all these authors (as,
according to our running hypothesis, he read Herbert and
Milton) but to him they can scarcely have been *authorities*. The
voice is here confessedly more Miltonic than divine. Once
again, there is a kind of inverse propriety in this. Negative
capability is all very well where one's fellow creatures are
concerned. With God, in a curious way, humility is better
served by the egotistical sublime. If we are to blame Herbert for
presuming to anticipate in words the moral essence of God's
love, let us be willing to praise Milton for adhering to the
gentlemanly reserve (before God) of humanist epic.

The conventions are so prominent, the style so patently
governed by human precedent, that there can be no mistaking
these lines for the real or even the probable thoughts of God
himself. But what of the justification of God? Did Milton, or
did he not, suppose that he was doing just that? Milton's
sterner ambitions were surely more than literary. Thus we find
ourselves at a stand. The style, we say, is savingly conventional.
The matter is literally assertive.

## II

## CONCRETENESS

In MILTON's project we may see both courage and a certain
conscious brutalism, characteristic of the later Renaissance. It
is sometimes suggested that through an inadvertent coarseness

of mind Milton failed to see that God must be wrapped in mystery and so committed the grand narrative *bêtise* of *Paradise Lost*. I question the inadvertency. Certainly *Paradise Lost* affronts with circumstantial narrative the proper obscurity of God. But the effrontery is surely deliberate. It may even be a genuine effect of integrity. Milton was consciously opposed to that theology which stresses the logical uniqueness of God and impatient with those who held that a being to whom no single epithet is literally applicable may nevertheless be described by analogy and metaphor. Thus, God, himself passionless, is said to be angry *from similitude of effect*. Milton wrote in his *De Doctrina Christiania*, I. ii,

> If it be said that 'he feared the wrath of the enemy', Deut. xxxii. 27, let us believe that it is not beneath the dignity of God to grieve in that for which he is grieved, or to be refreshed in that which refresheth him, or to fear in that he feareth. For however we may attempt to soften down such expressions by a latitude of interpretation, when applied to the Deity, it comes in the end to precisely the same.[2]

Here Milton's ostentatious coarseness has real point and power. We should not assume that all the intelligence is always on the side of those who acquiesce in a comfortable recession of metaphors. At the same time there is a latent subtlety in Milton's argument at this point to which we shall return later.

This deliberate literalism in theology finds in Milton its proper aesthetic correlative; that is, an aesthetic of apparent clarity, the Renaissance aesthetic of the great Florentine churches whose splendidly apprehensible interiors heroically defy the dim architectural sorcery of, say, St Mark's in Venice. To be sure, in Milton's verse the declaratory impulse exists in tension with an unsubdued ambiguity in the intimate texture of the lines as, at the level of subject matter, it wars with the darkness of Chaos. But the story is deliberately told in a declaratory and not a parabolic mode.

We live in an age in which such consciously achieved simp-

---

[2] In *The Works of John Milton*, ed. F. A. Patterson (The Columbia Milton), vol. XIV, trans. J. J. Hanford, New York, 1933, p. 35.

licities are not well received. In philosophy Hegelian idealism grows strong again and in the literary world the New Critical preference for polysemy and ambiguity persists. But Milton scorned any flinching from full assertion. And I for my part can honour that concreteness of mind which did not disdain to expound the nature of angelic excretion (v. 438).

Indeed the visit of Raphael, the eating, drinking, excreting angel in Book V, is the *locus classicus* for Miltonic literalism and physicalism. The tone is well set in the argument prefixed by Milton to this book:

> Raphael comes down to Paradise, his appearance described, his coming discerned by Adam afar off sitting at the door of his bower; he goes out to meet him, brings him to his lodge, entertains him with the choicest fruits of Paradise got together by Eve; their discourse at table.

Already the picture is a curious mixture of sublimity and what J. B. Broadbent has called 'good-tempered Flemish realism'.[3] Raphael approaches, six-winged, like Maia's son, all downy gold and colours dipped in Heaven, shaking his plumes as he walks. Adam sees him coming and calls out to Eve:

> Haste hither Eve, and worth thy sight behold
> Eastward among those trees, what glorious shape
> Comes this way moving; seems another morn
> Risen on mid-noon.
>
> (v. 308–11)

The last lines recall, and contrast with, the cancelled lines in the Trinity College Manuscript of *Comus*:

> Walks in black vapours, though the noontide brand
> Blaze in the summer solstice.
>
> (383–4)

Raphael is the opposite of the 'dark-souled' man and so, instead of darkness against light, we have a dazzling, eye-baffling superimposition of gold on gold, dawn on noon. But the splendour of the figure moving through the trees is joined to a strong sense of domesticity in the relation between Adam and

---

[3] *Some Graver Subject: An Essay on Paradise Lost*, 1960, p. 208.

Eve. Milton's marital dialogue not infrequently invites bathetic translation into common and familiar idiom. In Dalilah's words to Samson –

> In argument with men a woman ever
> Goes by the worse, whatever be her cause
>
> *(Samson Agonistes*, 903–4)

– one seems to hear the very accents of some sour exchange between Mr and Mrs Milton. So here Adam's words invite the translation: 'Hey, come and see something really worth seeing!' And at once the two of them begin to bustle about, exactly like any bourgeois couple surprised by a distinguished visitor. Even the wary thrift is there:

> Well we may afford
> Our givers their own gifts, and large bestow
> From large bestowed. . . .
>
> (316–18)

There is nothing like vicarious hospitality. Eve in reply eagerly explains that there is indeed plenty of everything, and in her eager optimism is so rash as to suggest that Raphael will have to agree that God's bounty on earth is no less than his bounty in heaven (329) – surely very dubious theology. Eve rapidly prepares a sort of Temperance Luncheon (strongly reminiscent of certain modern 'health food' cereals), consisting seemingly of fruit, berries and nuts, accompanied by unfermented grape-juice and creams pressed from nuts. This unalcoholic, uncooked meal has to appear rich and copious. To this task Milton the poet is entirely equal. His description is, so to speak, soberly sensuous, and Eve's hand as it heaps the food seems entirely generous.

Raphael is invited into the bower for a drink and (once more the 'low' translation has its limited appropriateness) replies that he has rather more than time for a quick one (376–7). What Milton delightfully called 'their discourse at table' then follows – 'no fear lest dinner cool'. Here at least we need not argue that a low translation is invited; the language is already low, and predictably was seized on by Richard Bentley as the handkerchief in *Othello* was seized on by Rymer.

At this point Adam experiences a most interesting form of hospitable disquiet:

> Heavenly stranger, please to taste
> These bounties which our nourisher, from whom
> All perfect good unmeasured out, descends,
> To us for food and for delight hath caused
> The earth to yield: *unsavoury food perhaps*
> *To spiritual natures.* . . .
>
> (397–404)

Raphael in reply explains from beginning to end the workings of his digestive system. He is a physical being, eats physical food, and 'what redounds transpires' (438).

Spirit and matter are not for Milton the radically opposed categories they were for Thomas Aquinas. Rather the universe is a continuum of more or less attenuated substance: emanations, influences, effulgences, exhalations, vapours, air, heat, aether: these are the modes, at once somehow physical and bodiless, which excite his imagination and nourish his theology. The context of all this is, as C. S. Lewis pointed out in his 'The Mistake about Milton's Angels',[4] post-Platonic Platonism. Dr Johnson had accused Milton of confusing matter and spirit. Lewis, in his anxiety to rebut this accusation, perhaps imparts too great a clarity to Milton's 'Platonic theology'. Lewis, with good authority, suggests that for the Platonists all *created* spirits are material. The creator is extra-material, but creation is essentially the imposition of form on *matter*. But whence came this matter? Milton notoriously held that it came from God's own substance: *creatio non ex nihilo sed ex suo*. Here he departed from strictly Platonic doctrine, for in the *Timaeus* matter is supposed to have existed from eternity and, as the source of all evil, to absolve God of any guilt with regard to the evident imperfections of creation. In *De Doctrina Christiana* I. vii,[5] Milton argues that the very notion of creation, in all the relevant languages, presupposes matter: it is a 'making out of something'. But if matter had not existed from eternity,

---

[4] *A Preface to Paradise Lost*, 1942, pp. 105–11.
[5] The Columbia Milton, vol. xv, p. 25.

matter itself must have been created. By the earlier argument, however, this creation also must have been from some *prior* matter. Milton does not make this awkward implication explicit, but it is fairly clear from his twists and turns that he felt its force. Taken rigidly (and Milton, as we have seen, had a taste for rigidity) the implication is that God is himself a material being; less rigidly, we might say that God is 'matter's matter', and allow ourselves to imagine the second as somehow more 'spiritual' than the first. Milton faces the challenge: 'It is objected, however, that body cannot emanate from spirit.' His answer seems in a manner to allow the force of the objection since he says, in effect, 'Yes indeed, but the alternative is even more absurd', or, in his actual words, 'I reply, much less can body emanate from nothing'. But within a few lines he feels strong enough to deny the minor premise (which I take to be, 'God is pure spirit' where 'spirit' means 'incorporeal substance'). He writes:

> Not even God's virtue and efficiency could have produced bodies out of nothing (as it is vulgarly believed he did) unless there had been some bodily force in his own substance, for no one can give something he has not got. And indeed, St. Paul himself did not hesitate to attribute something bodily to God, Col. ii. 9: *the whole fullness of the Godhead dwells in him bodily.*

The supposition seems to be that God's substance includes matter, but not as yet matter differentiated as such. He is willing, at the very least, to assert that in Aristotelian terms God must be the material cause of the universe. In *Paradise Lost* we find what looks at first like a much firmer assertion of the material nature of God, but then, once more, the thought seems to slip through our fingers:

> O Adam, one almighty is, from whom
> All things proceed, and up to him return,
> If not depraved from good, created all
> Such to perfection, one first matter all,
> Indued with various forms, various degrees
> Of substance, and in things that live, of life;

But more refined, more spirituous, and pure
As nearer to him placed or nearer tending
Each in their several active spheres assigned,
Till body up to spirit work, in bounds
Proportioned to each kind.

(v. 469–79)

Alistair Fowler sees in this the doctrine of *De Doctrina* I. vii
that God is the material cause of things. But Milton does not
quite say that. The 'one first matter' is not identified with God,
but rather with 'all' (one is tempted to write all things, but
Milton quite properly varies his chiastic echo to the truncated
'all', because 'things' are not, until form is imposed). At the
same time, in sympathy with Alistair Fowler, I find a fluidity in
the syntax here, a tendency to merge the flux of creation with
its end and source which may well express the theological view
Professor Fowler sets out. But, even if we grant so much,
Milton in a manner takes it from us when he seems to suggest
that the nearer a thing is to God the *less* material it is.

It is best to confess that the whole of this passage is pro-
foundly alien to the modern mind. To us a thing either is or is
not material. Smoke and air are, unequivocally, physical. *Heat*
is not for us closer than mind is, ontologically, to *circularity* (an
abstraction). But for Milton there is just such a continuum. The
Platonic extension of matter may yield occasional gross results
(like the passage on angelic digestion) but equally it can lead to
a curious 'spiritualization' of matter as we understand it. If a
modern analogy is sought, I offer the notion of mechanism. At
one time the idea that people may really be very complex
machines seemed a grotesque piece of reductionism. But the
apologists of mechanism gave such valid illustrations of the
startling capacities of machines that some of us began to think
that there was no longer any reason to fear the reduction of our
humanity since the machines themselves were now more
human than 'mechanical'. At least, there were times when it
seemed so. So in Milton the physicalism of his universe is, so to
speak, a transfigured and exalted physicalism.

Milton's address to light at the beginning of Book III illus-
trates his fluid apprehension of this question perfectly. Milton

begins by asking whether light was the first thing God created ('Let there be light') or whether it may have been co-eternal with God (here surely implying something like the Platonic doctrine that light is the divine emanation). The thought then brightens (so to speak) into a full assertion of the substantial identity of God and light:

> Since God is light,
> And never but in unapproached light
> Dwelt from eternity, dwelt then in thee,
> Bright effluence of bright essense increate.
>
> (III. 3–6)

But 'effluence' in line 6 is, once more, the Platonic doctrine. The modern reader infers that Milton is not talking about the sort of light that streams through his window on a June morning. But then he encounters lines 21–4:

> Thee I revisit safe,
> And feel thy sovereign vital lamp; but thou
> Revisit'st not these eyes, that roll in vain
> To find thy piercing ray, and find no dawn. . . .

This is real blindness; Milton knew. When in his desperate grief the poet prays for inward light, that he may

> See and tell
> Of things invisible to mortal sight
>
> (54–5)

we are no longer certain whether he is seeking something analogous to light, or light itself in another form or mode.

Readers of Milton have always (except perhaps for a brief period when the New Critics successfully repressed all knowledge of the poet's life) been moved by the tragic appropriateness of Milton to his task. It was right that the great poet who lost his sight should sing the loss of Paradise. But what to us is a tragic analogy may have been something more to Milton. In the invocation to Book III, Milton stretches out his hands to the light and to God, and no longer knows which is which.

At v. 573 Raphael speaks of 'likening spiritual to corporeal forms'. This to C. S. Lewis was the one (inconsistent) concession to those who believed that angels were immaterial. For the rest, he held, the poem was uniformly physicalistic. In fact, Raphael's words are only the most extreme of a number of passages in which some sort of contrast is drawn between bodily and spiritual things. But at the same time you can offer an angel a drink. Dr Johnson's claim that Milton repeatedly confuses spiritual and material things in *Paradise Lost* seems, as we (and Aristotle and Aquinas) understand those terms neither more nor less than the truth. We may answer that it is a learned, a *Platonic* confusion and we may with reason see in it a source of imaginative power rather than the debilitating influence proposed by Johnson, but on the central assertion of confusion I suspect that the Doctor was simply right.

The effect of this argument is, so to speak, to leaven the physicalism of Milton's universe, but to leave the literalism of his language unimpaired. Not only is God's fear something more than metaphor, 'God is light' is likewise something we are asked to try to take literally. Milton really thought that angels were somewhat as he described them and that God's reasons for doing what he did included the ones stated in the poem. When he thought of his human readers, he felt strong. He knew himself a match for any of them and in that mind could not help offering answers to the hardest questions. Thus for much of the time the only constraint on him is that the utterances of God and angels should be 'acceptable'. The obviously erroneous or intellectually vulnerable remark must never be placed in the mouth of an angel. This we may call a *literary* criterion. But when Milton thought of God at his elbow he felt weak. Among his peers he was willing to guess at the constitution of Heaven. Before God he has to confess that of himself he knew no more than he could glean from Scripture. Yet he cannot help himself; philosophize he must.

# III

## CURIOSITY

AT THE dangerous end of the meal (he has eaten well and relaxed) Adam broaches the question he feels he must ask of the angel:

> Thus when with meats and drinks they had sufficed,
> Not burdened nature, sudden mind arose
> In Adam, not to let the occasion pass
> Given him by this great conference to know
> Of things above his world, and of their being
> Who dwell in heaven, whose excellence he saw
> Transcend his own so far, whose radiant forms
> Divine effulgence, whose high power so far
> Exceeded human, and his wary speech
> Thus to the empyreal minister he framed.
>
> (451–60)

Here, surely, Adam is Milton. The itch to push things further, to enquire, not to miss a chance, to *know*, is unmistakable. But Adam, even in unbuttoned mood, is still wary, sensing that the knowledge he seeks may be forbidden. Dennis H. Burden has explained[6] how Milton in *Paradise Lost* was holding to a delicately balanced position with regard to the legitimacy of knowledge. Certain things man naturally knows, certain things he can be taught by a superior being, other things are the secrets of angels and there are at last some things known to God alone. Adam fears lest he should be asking to be let into secrets. In fact, Mr Burden reasons, everything is all right, as is shown by the angel's copious reply. Adam asks for and receives the sort of explanation which can properly be given to a man by an angel.

But what, meanwhile, must God think as he watches Milton

---

[6] *The Logical Epic: A Study of the Argument of Paradise Lost*, 1967, pp. 97–123.

write? Milton is not content to voice his human curiosity (this already involves presumption since unfallen curiosity was, one may suppose, an altogether higher thing) he is willing to write the reply given by the superior being. Milton doubtless thought or knew himself to be superior to other men but he did not doubt (did he?) that he was only a man. A technical solution of his problem might have been to confine himself strictly, in the angel's discourse, to Revelation and Scripture. Scripture, oddly enough, was not available to Adam and comes nearer than anything else to redressing the balance, in point of knowledge, between unfallen and fallen man. But Milton does not so confine himself. Instead we have a distinctively Miltonic physicalist metaphysic pronounced by an angel.

The truth is that Milton is not only present in Adam's curiosity; he is also present, and with the grossest superfluity, in the angel's answers. He had an itch to know and an even greater itch to lecture. One marvels at the shamelessness of it. At first we may be tempted to imagine that Milton must have muttered apologies to God as he wrote, much as an inexperienced lecturer in mathematics, on finding that a great mathematician had entered the room, might strive to signal his consciousness of inadequacy to the great man while he continued to read his prepared script to the class. But if this was true of Milton it left no imprint on the poem. He is commonly most aware of the real difficulties before he begins; there one finds the strange ambiguous appeals, half classical, half Christian, for inspiration, the careful statements of what may or may not be known. But the tide of exposition gathers strength and he forgets (it is hard not to assume this) his divine audience. Much as Galileo willingly agreed, when brought before the Inquisition, that his astronomy was merely hypothetical but when faced once more with an audience of students relapsed into positive assertion, so Milton plunges back from his brief acknowledgement of ignorance into profound confidence. In Book VII Adam once more grows inquisitive, and the angel says,

Yet what thou canst attain, which best may serve
To glorify the maker, and infer

Thee also happier, shall not be witheld
Thy hearing, such commission from above
I have received, to answer thy desire
Of knowledge within bounds.

(115–20)

This (though it already implies that man is to be told more than he *naturally* knows) is reasonably prudent. It shows some sense of Milton's real limitations as a human poet in the seventeenth century writing from earth. But within a few lines Raphael is providing a wealth of information, much of it nowhere to be found in Scripture. Similarly in Book VIII when Adam begins to ask astronomical questions, Raphael answers,

This to attain, whether heaven move or earth,
Imports not, if thou reckon right. . . .

(70–1)

And we note the prudence, on Milton's part. The technical literary problem is solved (the angel must not say anything which in ten years' time will look silly) and piety is preserved (Milton need not pretend to know more than he knows).

But Raphael and Milton cannot let the matter alone. The poet dwells in ever more loving detail on this realm, supposedly of no concern for man. Indeed the moral lines are strangely crossed. Adam's (human, Miltonic) curiosity is soberly rebuked by the angel and forthwith indulged, by the same angel. In the ancient figure of speech known as *occupatio* the speaker may lodge a given thing in his hearers' minds even while he pretends to disclaim all interest in it: 'I will not even bother to tell you how the late President robbed you all.' This of course is a deliberate trick. Raphael's speech seems instead a sort of *inadvertent occupatio*. The expression on Adam's face must have been interesting: presumably submissive acceptance of Raphael's refusal mingled with an eager vigilance for whatever is going after all to slip through the bars of that refusal.

But Milton, before he undertook these passages, asked for inspiration. May he not have considered, as the thoughts rose in his mind, that his prayer had been answered? If Milton was inspired then God wrote Raphael's speeches and our com-

( 96 )

plaints are silenced. But I doubt whether even Milton could believe that this was truly so. In all the great invocations of the poem, in Book I, Book III and Book VII, there is a kind of doubleness, a hesitation, which betrays much. At the very beginning of the poem Milton calls first upon the heavenly Muse and later on the Holy Spirit. These, it seems clear, are conceived as substantially distinct. Dame Helen Gardner has drawn our attention[7] to the marked change in tone as Milton turns from the passionate invocation of his literary and Biblical heritage to direct prayer. In the address to Urania at the beginning of Book VII the duality persists, but seems less marked. Milton affirms that his Urania is not one of the nine Muses, that she lived before the hills were made, conversing with eternal Wisdom in the presence of the almighty Father. Further, he tells us, it is 'The meaning, not the name I call' (VII, 5). This, as Lily B. Campbell has written,[8] is 'la Muse Chrestienne' of Du Bartas. The step from this conception to that of the Holy Spirit is now small indeed. And yet still the presence of all that loved, not-yet-quite-rejected pagan matter in the lines exerts its powerful gravitational pull. The poet remembers Olympus as he soars above it, remembers Pegasus as he outstrips his flight. Once again we have that strange literary phenomenon, the inadvertent *occupatio*.

In any case, if the call for divine inspiration were deemed to have been effective, what need for these defensive preliminaries from Raphael? Milton must have been aware as he wrote that *he* did not know for sure whether Copernicus was wrong, while God most certainly was quite clear on the subject.

As for the most powerful and the most mysterious of the invocations, the prelude to Book III, that we have already discussed. The tension between a loved literary heritage and a longed-for visitation of the Spirit is now replaced by a more urgent juxtaposition: remembered sunlight and the creator of the world. But neither of these is given back to him. The inspiration of Adam was endless until he fell. But Milton is fallen. The very subject of the poem is in a manner opposed to

---

[7] *A Reading of Paradise Lost*, 1965, pp. 18–20.
[8] 'The Christian Muse', *Huntingdon Library Bulletin*, VII, 1935, pp. 29–70.

the idea of easy commerce with God; for this poem is about Milton's blindness, not his sight, and about the loss of Paradise.

## IV

# THE THEORY OF ACCOMMODATION

MILTON's theory of accommodation is sometimes produced as a means of resolving all our difficulties over the poet's presumption. Milton, we are told, accommodates his matter to the understanding of his audience. Hence the physicalism, the 'hard' imagery, the domesticity of Adam and Eve, the confident dialogue with angels and the Trinity. Nothing is supposed real; it is a package, of artificially manageable propositions. In fact Milton's theory of accommodation as set forth in the *De Doctrina Christiana* is at once subtler and much more original than the above version suggests. To begin with, 'accommodation' is practised, not by poets, but by God himself:

God is known, so far as he is pleased to make us acquainted with himself, either from his own nature, or from his efficient power.

When we speak of knowing God, it must be understood with reference to the imperfect comprehension of man; for to know God as he really is, far transcends the powers of man's thoughts, much more of his perception. . . .

Our safest way is to form in our minds such a conception of God, as shall correspond with his own delineation and representation of himself in the sacred writings. For granting that both in the literal and figurative descriptions of God, he is exhibited not as he really is, but in such a manner as may be within the scope of our comprehension, yet we ought to entertain such a conception of him, as he, in condescending to accommodate himself to our capacities, has shown that he desires we should conceive.[9]

[9] *De Doctrina Christiana*, I, ii, in the Columbia Milton, vol. XIV, pp. 31–3.

I have quoted from the *De Doctrina Christiana* the passage in which Milton defends a literal understanding of God's 'fear' and the like. We are now in a position to see that this 'plain man' approach issues from an exceedingly complex and carefully defended position. To say that God 'feared the wrath of the enemy' (Deut. 32: 27) is to describe *literally* a semblance produced by God himself. The 'accommodated God' conveyed in Scripture is itself part of the fabric of objective reality and is susceptible of literal description. Indeed it is peculiarly amenable to literal description since it is expressly designed for human comprehension. As it stands the theory is an immensely clever specimen of philosophical radicalism. It condemns the remote Scholastic for essaying a knowledge of God at odds with the picture presented in Scripture by God himself, and it gives divine authority to the conceptions of the simple peasant. Perhaps, by the same token, it authorizes retrospectively the grossest familiarities of *Paradise Lost*?

In fact, as we have seen, *Paradise Lost* does not restrict itself to the images of God presented to the simple in Scripture. A great deal of the higher Scholasticism gets into the poem. And indeed the theory itself is shot through with the same contradiction. You cannot invoke a sophisticated theory to commend simplicity and then forget that you were once sophisticated. If God were known to us only as he has accommodated himself to our conceptions, there could be no 'theory of accommodation'. If we had no inkling of a larger, more mysterious God, how could we ever suspect that an accommodation had taken place? If Milton really supposed that *Paradise Lost* dealt with the 'accommodated God' only, the poem becomes, in a curious manner, *faux-naif*.

Even as he states the theory, Milton betrays himself by hesitations. He is at first confident that we do not know God 'as he really is' (p. 31). The semblance presented by God is, it would appear, a false one. This would in turn imply that in so far as 'God feared' belongs with the accommodated version of God, it is simply untrue. God did not *really* fear the enemy at all. Yet Milton says we must as men believe that he did because that is what he wants us to believe. It seems clear that one of us at least is not doing what he was told. A little later however

Milton offers the truth of the 'semblance' as an open question:

In a word, God either is, or is not, such as he represents himself to be. If he be really such, why should we think otherwise of him? If he be not such, on what authority do we say what God has not said?[10]

It might seem that the answer is plain. If God is exactly as he represents himself the 'theory of accommodation' falls to the ground; no accommodation has occurred; if on the other hand he is not such as he represents himself to be then, once we understand this, it is only through (of all things) a sort of pious bad faith that we can continue to believe what is evidently untrue. A solution might have been to suggest that the 'accommodated picture' is a part but not the whole of the truth, but Milton does not clearly adopt it.

One is left with an uneasy sense that *Paradise Lost* may indeed be faithfully literal, but faithfully literal to what? To a divinely authorized semblance of an inaccessible truth. When we say to Milton, 'Surely you don't think God is like *that*?' he has his answer ready: 'No, of course not, but that is what He wants one to say.' The picture is repulsive and it is a relief to discover that we need not accept it. For it is plain that, as there are two orders in Milton's religious thought, that which speaks simply of the fears and griefs of God and that which provides a transcendant justification for that very simplicity, so in his poem there are the picturesque conceptions and the metaphysical. The theory of accommodation, we have seen, could not have occurred to a mind wholly confined to the accommodated presentation. Much of *Paradise Lost* belongs to the higher, unconfined order of metaphysical thought. The doctrine of God as a highly rarefied material cause is no part of the accommodated picture; nor was the project of 'justification'.

[10] *ibid.*, p. 37.

# V

## JUSTIFICATION

To show the justice of God's ways to man, Milton took an aetiological myth, a story purporting to account for the introduction of evil into a universe governed by an all-good, all-powerful God. He treated the story seriously, as what really happened, as something which could really explain the presence of evil in the world. And, as many readers have perceived, he found that the explanatory structure of his narrative would not hold.

The basic premises seemed at first to be strong. Adam fell because he was free. 'Free' *means* that he *could* divagate from the will of God. He did so divagate and – 'there's an end on't'. But such formulae seldom survive a detailed narrative exposition. If Adam and Eve were created good they would *spontaneously* have followed God's will in everything they did. To depart from God's will would be to misuse one's freedom, and this they could have done only if they were already tainted.

Thus the aetiological myth presupposes the very thing it purports to explain. This, indeed, seems to be characteristic of myths about the origin of evil or guilt. For example, Freud's account[11] of guilt and morality as originating with the murder of the father by the jealous sons is open to the same criticism. Why should the sons, on that primal occasion, have felt guilt unless they were, already, moral beings? Grief mingled with exultant pride one could understand, but why guilt? Only a twilit intelligence can rest content with a story which seeks to explain the beginning of something merely by recounting a simple series from an arbitrary first term: 'How did ships begin?' 'There was a man called Jason and he built the first ship, and he sailed over the sea' and so forth.

In the case of *Paradise Lost* the situation is complicated by a

---

[11] In *Totem and Taboo*, iv: 5, and in *Civilisation and its Discontents*, vii; in *The Complete Psychological Works of Sigmund Freud*, ed. J. Strachey, vol. XIII, 1955, p. 142 and vol. XII, 1961, pp. 131–3.

curious effect of reduplication in the myth. Before Adam fell Lucifer fell, so that, if, unsatisfied by a mere reference to freedom, we persist in asking why Adam fell, an answer is ready: he was pushed. Though evil was not yet among men it already lived on the other side of Chaos. If, however, the fall of Adam is not intelligible without the previous fall of Lucifer, we are bound to ask, 'How then did Lucifer fall?' He 'thought himself impaired', says Milton (v. 665) at the anointing of the Son. Is this, then, the real origin of evil in the universe? But Satan must have been bad *already* to feel so resentful. Once again the evil is presupposed by the very story which purports to explain it.

And in any case the story of Adam and Eve continues to perplex. If Adam fell only because he was pushed, then he did nothing wrong and evil did not at that point find a way into the human race. If, on the other hand, his will consented, he must have been corrupt already, and so forth, as before.

There are some who hold that the detailed narrative of Book IX is a miracle of psychological analysis, a subtle exploration of the beginnings of evil in the human soul. I will not dissent from this view. I will only observe that it is a fallacy – in fact, the naturalistic fallacy – to suppose that any amount of *psychological* analysis will ever tell you anything at all about the intrinsic character of evil. Milton's mind was admirably fitted to perceive this sort of stark and basic truth. Thus, through all the multiplication of incident, all the narrative sophistication of the original myth even to the brilliant stroke (in Book IV) of causing Satan to approach Eve through her Unconscious (toad-like at her ear while she slept) the same questions persist. If Eve was morally wrong to disobey Adam and go off by herself, then evil already existed in Eden. If on the other hand Eve was not responsible for her Unconscious, she committed no sin when her Unconscious received the suggested of Satan and moral evil has yet to be introduced. If conversely she could to some extent control her Unconscious and was thus responsible for its operations, she must have been already corrupt to consent so to the suggestions of Satan.

I am aware that the theological worries I have just run through are both primitive and out-moded. I suppose the line of thought represented is that of a fairly bright schoolboy of sixteen. But in a way their very simplicity is essential to the case I am trying to make. It is sometimes said that thoughts of this sort could never have occurred to anyone before the Romantic movement. I answer: thoughts as primitive as this could occur to anyone. We cannot be certain that they did not occur to Milton. Naturally Augustine picked this up:

> Our first parents fell into open disobedience because already they were secretly corrupted; for the evil act had never been done had not an evil will preceded it.[12]

I have a further reason for offering these arguments here. Although I have seen many very intricate refutations of these objections I have never seen one in which I could begin to believe.

But, if a more elaborate example is wanted, take the Argument to Book V: 'God to render man inexcusable sends Raphael to admonish him of his obedience, of his free estate, of his enemy near at hand.' The words seem to say that God 'framed' Adam, or illicitly tricked him into guilt. The usual explanation is that 'to render man inexcusable' is a sort of short-hand for 'in order to make sure that Adam's action was morally significant, to make sure that, if he made the wrong decision, he did so in the light of full information and therefore inexcusably.' Because God foreknew that Adam would in fact choose wrong, we are given 'to render inexcusable' rather than the neutral 'to render significant'. Meanwhile the literary reader, trained to mistrust paraphrase, may still wonder at the expression Milton chose actually to use. The poet has chosen a form of words which tactlessly obtrudes the fact that a God who foreknows a certain action and takes steps to ensure the occurrence of that action is in a certain sense a cause of that action, and withal morally responsible. The stronger our sense of interconnected chronological order in these events the stronger will be our sense of God as in this case the author or joint-author of evil. And to those who accuse us of anachron-

---

[12] *City of God*, Book XIV: 13, in the translation by Marcus Dods, Edinburgh, 1872, vol. II, p. 25.

ism we may point out that in these words Milton, usually far from docile to Calvin's teaching, actually echoes the master:

The purpose of natural law, therefore, is to render man inexcusable.[13]

And Calvin, as we have seen, has a way of meaning what he says.

One way of coping with the difficulty (and there is some warrant for it in the poem) is to invoke the doctrine of the *felix culpa* or Happy Fall. This transforms the apparent evil of Adam's fall into a mysterious good, so that God in procuring that fall was really exerting his love all the time. This, it would seem, is one of those doctrines which we are meant to glimpse in moments of distress and not to contemplate steadily. For if we take it seriously it subverts the very foundations of ordinary Christian belief. The change, to put it mildly, is considerable: the greatest evil that ever befell man was really the greatest good. The punishment for Adam's sin was the first stage in a *promotion*.

The best theological answer is Boethius'. God is outside time and the impression we have of serial order in his actions and thoughts is an illusion. God's foreknowledge of an event certainly *entails* the occurrence of that event but it does not force it to happen; similarly my knowledge that William is sitting there *entails* that William should sit there but does not force him to do so.[14] This Milton gratefully adopted ('If I foreknew, foreknowledge had no influence on their fault', III, 116–17). But we should notice the effect it has on the allied thesis: 'Adam fell

[13] *Institutes of the Christian Religion*, II. ii. 22, ed. J. T. McNeill, trans. Ford Lewis Battles Vol. 1, p. 282. Norton (1561) writes, 'that man may be made inexcusable'. The French text, however, is very close: 'La fin donc de la Loy naturelle, est de rendre l'homme inexcusable', *Institution de la religion chrestienne*, texte de la première édition française (1541) ed. A. Lefranc, H. Chatelain and J. Pannier, Bibliotheque de l'École des Hautes Études, Paris, 1911, p. 61. The Latin text is *ut reddatur homo inexcusabilis*, in *Ioannis Calvini opera quae supersunt omnia*, ed. G. Baum, E. Cunitz and E. Reuss, vol. II, Braunschweig, 1863, p. 204.
I owe this reference to Mr Michael Keefer.
[14] See the *Consolatio Philosophiae*, v. iii, in *Boethius, The Theological Treatises*, with an English translation by H. F. Stewart and E. K. Rand, 1962, pp. 374f.

because he was free.'). If Boethius' argument is fresh in our minds we shall find it hard to accept that 'because', as it stands. At once we find ourselves wanting to say, 'Freedom *entails* the possibility of Adam's fall, but it in no way *causes* him to fall.' In other words, we can only pretend that Adam's freedom *explains* his fall as long as we conflate the notions of entailment and causation. But this is what Boethius has expressly forbidden us to do. If we insist, against Boethius, that entailment is a sort of cause, we are forthwith forced to admit that, in so far as God foreknew Adam's sin, he caused it, and is therefore the author of evil. After all, freedom entails only the possibility and not the necessary occurrence of the fall, but foreknowledge, on the other hand, directly entails the fact of sin. The entailment in the second case is, so to speak, 'tighter'. Thus *a fortiori* God's foreknowledge caused the sin of Adam *more certainly* than Adam's freedom caused his fall.

Moreover the proposition that freedom entails the possibility of divagation from the will of God is itself internally disputable, by a parallel process of reasoning. A man is 'unfree' only if the possibility of his going astray is stopped by some force. If it is merely precluded by *entailment*, for example, if Adam's perfect goodness *entailed* the fact that he could not sin, then his freedom would remain unimpaired.

We should notice that the effect of Boethius' reasoning is to emancipate theology from the order of temporal narrative and to transpose it to a higher order of abstraction. I am tempted to say, following the *De Doctrina Christiana*, that if Milton says that God rendered man inexcusable, let us believe that Milton meant that God rendered man inexcusable.

Meanwhile there are other difficulties, less abstruse in character While God's behaviour, subjected to a narrative causal sequence, appears increasingly unacceptable, so at a more emotional level the reader's sympathies notoriously go wrong. The Devil in his war on Heaven attracts our sympathy. Adam, at the moment which brought death into the world and all our woe, attracts our sympathy. In each case theological answers are available. Should we therefore sympathize with God? God's inscrutable love and power are beyond the reach of such cosy emotions. Had Milton made God a 'sympathetic' character his error would have been worse. But must the converse hold? Must evil be so alluring?

We would be heart and soul on God's side, but the story *qua* story does not make it easy for us. I see no reason to date this feeling from the romantics, though they were the first to give it powerful utterance. In Milton, the theologian of divine Matter, the poet of vast darknesses and gigantic forms, the celebrant of energy, they correctly perceived a kindred spirit. But the narrative effect I have in mind is at least as old as *Jack the Giant-killer*. Since only the weak or the out-numbered can be brave it follows that heroic literature must exalt the imperilled and the doomed. It cannot, by its very nature, praise a virtue 'without dust and heat', cloistered in omnipotence. Mr Vincent Crummles, no wild romantic but a practical man of business, explained the matter very clearly to Nicholas Nickleby (who found the broad-sword combat between the tall boy and the short boy somewhat ill-matched): if 'the sympathies of the audience' are to be got up 'in a legitimate manner', there must be a short one, and he must win.[15]

It was of course unthinkable that a Christian poet in the seventeenth century should explicitly espouse the cause of Satan. But there was no need for Milton to do so. The *story* did so of itself. Moreover there is in the shadowy antecedents of *Paradise Lost* something which would more particularly tend to make Satan and not God the hero of the work.

It seems that *Paradise Lost* existed in Milton's mind as a kind of Greek tragedy before it became an epic.[16] Greek tragedy owes its special force to the stratified coexistence of two ethical worlds. The older stratum is one in which men delighted in the unimpeded energy and even the bragging of the archaic heroes: in the later stratum men view such behaviour not precisely as sinful but as peculiarly likely to attract the jealous anger of the gods. Thus Greek tragedy is not typically concerned with evil men who get what they deserve but is rather about heroes (Ajax, Heracles, Eteocles and Polynices) whose very super-

[15] Charles Dickens, *Nicholas Nickleby*, ch. XXII.
[16] See the four drafts in the Trinity College Manuscript, and Edward Phillips, *The Life of Mr. John Milton*, 1694, in *The Early Lives of Milton*, ed. Helen Darbishire, 1932, p. 72.

fluity of energy offends the infinitely more powerful gods. The element of heroic theomachy, of war waged by men against gods, though prudently veiled in the tragedies themselves and doubtless destined to be rebutted in Milton's projected tragedy, is nevertheless discernible by the imagination still.

That Milton went to the ancient world, not in a spirit of docile imitation but rather as its schoolmaster, to correct and discipline its moral vagaries, need not destroy this presentiment of tension. After all in *Comus*[17] (the very word means 'masque' or 'revel') he entered the world of masque in order to dethrone its ancient King, and yet in the end the old wild law of masque would have its way. Comus is defeated, not by Grace or Reason, but by another Nature Spirit; the Lady had feared to come upon some

> ll-managed merriment,
> Such as the jocund flute, or gamesome pipe
> Stirs up among the loose unlettered hinds,
> When for their teeming flocks, and granges, full
> In wanton dance they praise the bounteous Pan,
> And thank the gods amiss.
>
> (171–6)

Yet she is at last restored to her father with just such a festive ritual

> As Mercury did first devise
> With the mincing Dryades
> On the lawns, and on the leas.
>
> (962–4)

The only world which the *poem* would accept as the environment proper to innocence is one which Milton's Puritanism had sought to reject as unregenerate. So with *Paradise Lost*, the very poem will not permit God to be hero, for the general reason that he is unfitted for the role by his omnipotence and for the more particular reason that a smell of Greek tragedy still hangs in the air. That Milton was aware of this

---

[17] The work itself ('a Masque presented at Ludlow Castle') was not known as *Comus* until 1738, when John Dalton adapted it for the stage.

artistic difficulty, as any competent artist must in any age be aware, is shown by his contriving the episode of Abdiel, 'among the faithless, faithful only he' (v. 897). Milton knew that he must show *virtue* in danger, out-numbered, but, with the big battalions so present to our imagination, the effort is not very successful. If little can be done for Abdiel, less can be done for God, who though only one (or perhaps three) is also infinite and cannot lose. Even the Crucifixion was a self-inflicted wound and another kind of triumph.

## VI

## TELLING STORIES ABOUT GOD

C. S. LEWIS wrote that to complain that the War in Heaven is uninteresting because a foregone conclusion is to miss the point, since between God and Satan there can be no war at all. There is a war between Satan and Michael, and it is stopped. But between God and the Devil, he explains, the difference is not military but metaphysical. Once again the argument deftly lifts our subject out of the reach of narrative. For *stories* are of wars. If you wish to express a metaphysical division as a story, you will find yourself telling the story of a war, and, if you are then rebuked for confounding a metaphysical and a physical opposition, your only course is to confess that trying to tell a story was a mistake. In a way C. S. Lewis conceded as much, when he wrote,

> The cosmic story – the ultimate *plot* in which all other stories are episodes – is set before us. We are invited, for the time being, to look at it from outside. And that is not, in itself, a religious exercise. When we remember that we also have our places in this plot, that we also at any given moment, are moving either towards the Messianic or towards the Satanic position, then we are entering the world of religion. But when we do that, our epic holiday is over: we rightly shut up our Milton. In the religious life man faces God and God faces

man. But in the epic it is feigned, for the moment, that we, as readers, can step aside and see the faces both of God and man in profile.[18]

It will be noticed that Lewis at the moment when he writes 'we also' is on the brink of carrying out what I have called 'a reflexive check'. But then he draws a careful artificial line: there is fiction and there is reality. Much, however, is conceded in his admission that the poet only 'feigns' that he can see God in profile. Certainly it seems that whenever the story begins to give God as character that degree of substance which narrative naturally seeks to confer, we encounter instead of substance a hiatus, created by the logical uniqueness of God, a uniqueness which resists all ordinary characterization by behaviour and consequence. It is as if at any level below the metaphysical the ideas of God and a third person grammar are mutually antithetical. Thus God is not 'he' but, essentially, 'thou', just as, in relation to him, all human beings are not 'they' but 'we' (or, individually, 'I').

It would seem then that it is idle to look in *Paradise Lost* for a God who is the source and object of all love. Any literature which is properly cognisant of this truth will reflect the intuition in its very grammar, which will naturally modulate from third to second person, and will approach the divine mystery not by substantives but rather by whispered vocatives. Thus Dante in his *Commedia* preserves the narrative mode for everything except God. When in the last canto of the *Paradiso* poet and pilgrim become one (there was never more between them than the narrative fiction) Dante addresses God directly

> O luce etterna che sola in te sidi

> O Light Eternal, that alone abidest in Thyself.[19]
>
> (XXXIII. 124)

We may even carry this analysis back to pre-Christian times, but only, I think, as far as Virgil. Virgil decided to write the

---

[18] *Preface to Paradise Lost*, 1942, p. 132.
[19] Text and translation from *The Divine Comedy of Dante Alighieri*, with translation and comment by John D. Sinclair, 1958.

*Iliad* and the *Odyssey* all over again, with Aeneas for hero, falling between Troy and Rome, and so created by typology and lineage a Homeric epic of Roman history. It is commonly conceded that this decision marks one of the great miracles of literary organization, the virtual creation of a poetry of imaginative interpenetration, *idem in alio*, of a sympathetic cosmos and a significantly ordered history. Yet at one point the structure gapes pitifully.

The Homeric apparatus of merry gods and goddesses resists translation to that sadder Italian sky. Their wrangles are faithfully reworked by Virgil, are given a high, declamatory polish, but they have no power to move us. And yet the *Aeneid* is a great religious poem. The religion, in fact, is all in the praying human subjects, none in the blandly displayed divinities. The great gap of the *Aeneid* is between the prayers of Aeneas and his dispossessed followers and the discourse of the Olympians. *Those* prayers cannot, we feel, be directed to *these* gods. And of course the prayers are in the second person. But a God addressed 'in whispered vocatives' suggests nothing so strongly as George Herbert, and we saw what happened to him.

If God is listening Milton is in trouble. In God's hearing he undertook to show that God's ways are just. This is already mildly embarrassing. He proceeded (in Book III) to write a form of self-justification to be pronounced by God himself: which is more embarrassing. He was, however, in part defended by the conventions of epic narrative, which remind the reader at every point that what he has before him is a human construct. This is the signal difference between Milton and Herbert. But, even while the narrative mode protected Milton, it was bringing him into great danger. For, as we have seen, the mere impetus of detailed narration forces the asking of questions, the airing of doubts, the subversion of sympathies. Thus it was that Milton not only undertook, in God's hearing, the defence of God, but found as he wrote that God seemed indefensible. This is not so much embarrassing as terrifying. For there can be no question, I think, of a saving atheism coming to Milton at this point. God continued to watch, but what kind of a God was it that now sat staring from the shadows? Dame Helen Gardner says that Milton 'surely

. . . took for granted that God was by definition, good.'[20] In my experience people say 'surely' when they are not in fact sure. I for my part can be sure of no such thing. I have already suggested that the thought that God may be evil may have occurred to many of the more attentive readers of Calvin. That it should be seldom expressed is scarcely surprising. In view of the vigilance of God doubtless many would have striven to suppress it even in their own minds. But if I am asked how I can even have lighted upon a phenomenon so pertinaciously concealed even from contemporaries, the answer is simple. It is implied logically by Calvin's argument and it is betrayed implicitly in the poetry of Milton and Herbert.

Jonathan Richardson tells a curiously sour tale of Milton's old age. As in Shakespearian comedy noble lovers are mirrored by peasant lovers, so in Milton's household the great Puritan had for a servant a Puritan zealot. Richardson writes,

> *Milton* had a Servant, who was a very Honest, Silly, Fellow, and a Zealos and Constant Follower of these Teachers; when he came from the Meeting his Master would frequently Ask him What he had heard, and Divert Himself with Ridiculing Their Fooleries, or (it may be) the Poor Fellow's Understanding; both One and t'other Probably; However This was so Grievous to the Good Creature, that he left his Service upon it.[21]

Toland says[22] that Milton in his last years attended no religious assembly, and would make use of no established rite in his own household. It is not always noticed by modern readers that the picture presented here is, to say the least, unusual. One wonders how – and even if – the ageing Milton prayed.

[20] *A Reading of Paradise Lost*, p. 26.
[21] *Explanatory Notes and Remarks on Milton's Paradise Lost, with a Life of the Author*, 1734, in *The Early Lives of Milton*, p. 238.
[22] *The Life of John Milton*, 1698, in ibid., p. 195.

# III. THE THIRD CANTO
# OF THE PARADISO

## THE MOON PEOPLE

Quel sol che pria d'amor mi scaldò'l petto,
  di bella verità m'avea scoverto,
  provando e riprovando, il dolce aspetto. . . .

That sun which first warmed my breast
  with love had discovered to me, by proof and
  refutation, fair truth's sweet aspect. . . .[1]

DANTE has entered Paradise and been conducted to the
Heaven of the Moon, where are to be found those whose
faithfulness was marred by inconstancy. Dante begins his
canto with the blazing image of the sun. He has already
invoked Apollo, the sun god, at I. 13 and II. 8, but Apollo, thus
mythologized, is a remoter thing than 'Quel sol', and was in my
case invoked less for light than for his poetic patronage. This
sun is Beatrice, the little girl in the red dress with whom Dante
fell irremediably in love at the age of nine, now transfigured in
Paradise. She, the unblemished sun, has just explained to Dante
the spots we see on the moon.

[1] *Paradiso*, III. 1–3. All Dante quotations, both Italian and English, are from
*The Divine Comedy of Dante Alighieri*, with translation and comment by
John D. Sinclair, 1958.

Already the poetry has begun to work, preparing our imagination to receive the dim beatitude of those whose love was touched by weakness. They are the blemished yet still heavenly moon to Beatrice's more heavenly sun. Dante turns from the solar clarity of Beatrice's words to something strange and confusing to his eyes. Before he turned, he had embarked upon a courteous acknowledgement of Beatrice's lesson, but the sight which usurped his attention silenced his tongue. It is characteristic of Paradisal experience in Dante that by an overlapping action it should cancel the assertion, however exemplary, of the poet's personal self. Again and again he is surprised into self-oblivion. What he sees is indeed strange:

> Quali per vetri trasparenti e tersi,
>   O ver per acque nitide e tranquille,
>   non sì profonde che i fondi sien persi,
> tornan di nostri visi le postille
>   debili sì, che perla in bianca fronte
>   non vien men tosto alle nostre pupille;
> tali vid'io più facce a parlar pronte;
>   per ch'io dentro all error contrario corsi
>   a quel ch'accese amor tra l'omo e'l fonte.
>
> (10–18)

As through smooth and transparent glass, or
through limpid and still water not so deep
that the bottom is lost, the outlines of our faces
return so faint that a pearl on a white brow
does not come less quickly to our eyes, many
such faces I saw, eager to speak; at
which I ran into the opposite error to that
which kindled love between the man and the spring.

It is likely that glass which Dante would describe as *trasparente* would strike a twentieth-century person as dim. The best glass of the time was thus. 'Water not so deep that the bottom is lost' likewise does not suggest complete and detailed visibility. Similarly the image of the pearl on the lady's brow, white on almost-white, with its substitution of a chromatic blurring for the more common use of heightening contrast, is a muted version of what Milton was later to do in his 'gold on gold' description of Raphael (v. 310f.). Dante's lines are a subtler, moderated form of this 'invisible through excess of light' paradox, of which he makes full use elsewhere. This paradox is itself destined to be turned inside out by Dante at XXXIII. 77, where he says that if he were to look *away* from the light his eyes would dazzle. Here it is still the sight itself which confuses his eye, not however by its brilliance but by a softer commingling of white with less than white.

The sense of a difficulty which is extreme and yet resolvable is reflected in the complex structure of the sentences. Of course Dante always enjoys, apparently for its own sake, the purely formal difficulty created by allusion and periphrasis. For 'in summer' he writes, 'in that season of the year when the sun least hides his face from us'. Here in the third canto, however, the lamination of negatives serves a further purpose. We 'peer' with our minds as Dante peered with his eyes, first at *non sì profonde*, 'not so deep', then at *non vien men tosto*, 'does not come less quickly' and at last at the still more intricate *io dentro all' error contrario corsi la quel ch' accese amor tra l'omo e'l fonte*, 'I ran into the opposite error to that which kindled love between the man and the spring'. Dante means, we gradually learn, that while Narcissus mistook a reflection for reality, he (Dante) mistook reality for a mere reflection.

Yet Dante will not let us rest too soon; he interposes a further difficulty. In a way it is the Miltonic problem of 'accommodation' all over again. In the following canto Beatrice explains to Dante that Piccarda and Constance are not really in the sphere of the moon at all. They are shown thus to Dante, accommodated to his sensuous apprehension (for by no other means could he understand that their rank is lower than that of other dwellers in Paradise). In fact all dwell in the same heaven. Thus one is tempted to say that Dante's first impression was perfectly correct. What he took for a reflection was indeed a mere image. But this will not do. What he saw was really there for him to see, ordained by God. It was not a mere reflection of some other sensuous reality but on the contrary was the one sensuous presentation available. And, after the manner ordained for him, he really saw Piccarda and Constance. The divine accommodation of their forms shimmers as reflections do on earth, yet is at once more substantial than a reflection and less than the full reality (which Dante could not comprehend).

The movement from thought to substance, which began with the overlapping of Dante's answer to Beatrice by the sight of the other faces, now receives a profounder formulation. Again Dante's personal self is cancelled by a larger reality, in that his error is replaced by the truth, and at the same time a type of the merely self-indulgent use of imagination is supplied in the figure of Narcissus. Beatrice (such is the laughter of Paradise) laughs to see him so confounded, not so much in derision at the error as in delight at the solution. Hobbes thought laughter arose from a perception of one's own 'sudden glory' in comparison with others.[2] Beatrice laughs not at her own but at *Dante's* sudden glory.

## II

# THE TRANSFORMATION OF NARCISSUS

DANTE, unlike Narcissus, took real faces for an illusion. The imaginative movement from image to reality can produce a strange shiver in the mind. It may be that there is latent in it the strange force of Anselm's ontological proof. We have already referred briefly to this proof in our discussion of 'the reflexive check', by which the critic allows reality to intrude upon fiction (as by asking, 'But what of the man himself, as he writes this?'). This time we must allow Anselm to speak for himself:

> Now we believe that thou art a being than which none greater can be thought. . . . It is one thing for an object to be in the understanding and another to understand that it

[2] In *Human Nature*, 1650, ch. IX; in *The English Works of Thomas Hobbes*, ed. Sir William Molesworth, vol. IV, 1840, p. 46.

exists. When a painter considers beforehand what he is going to paint, he has it in his understanding, but he does not suppose that what he has not yet painted already exists. But when he has painted it, he both has it in his understanding and understands that what he has now produced exists. Even the fool, then, must be convinced that a being than which none greater can be thought exists at least in his understanding, since when he hears this he understands it, and whatever is understood is in the understanding. But clearly that than which a greater cannot be thought cannot exist in the understanding alone. For if it is actually in the understanding alone, it can be thought of as existing also in reality, and this is greater. Therefore, if that than which a greater cannot be thought is in the understanding alone, this same thing than which a greater cannot be thought is that than which a greater can be thought. But obviously this is impossible. Without doubt, therefore, there exists, both in the understanding and in reality, something than which a greater cannot be thought.[3]

Anselm argues from the premise that a thing which really exists is obviously greater (that is, richer or better) than a mere mental image or conception. He points out that if you join this proposition (with which many people could agree) to the definition of God as 'that than which nothing greater can be thought', it follows that God must already *have* existence, for otherwise we could 'think' him greater, by mentally attributing real existence to him.

To most readers the argument seems mere unmeaning sound. To trained philosophers (like Bertrand Russell[4]) the argument is powerful, and urgently requires refutation. This has, of course, been supplied by a host of philosophers from Aquinas to Kant and after. Meanwhile there remains a smaller group who find beneath the stiff scholastic surface of the prose a kind of magic, something which can haunt at one and the same time the imagination and the intellect. This arises from the fact that the argument moves in an almost miraculous

[3] *Proslogion*, ch. II, in vol. X, *Anselm to Ockham*, ed. and trans. E. R. Fairweather, The Library of Christian Classics, 1956, pp. 73–4.
[4] See his *History of Western Philosophy*, 1946, p. 438.

fashion from concept to fact. From a mere definition, from a theoretical agreement on working notions, it extracts a reality, or seems to do so. The argument, even while it draws a severe distinction between concept and reality, succeeds in finding in one particular *concept*, the *open* concept *according* to which God is greater than we can conceive, God's real *existence*. What we took for a reflection was in fact a real face, anxious for speech.

Dante may have known the *Cur Deus Homo* of Anselm and, just possibly, the *De Similitudinibus*. I see no reason to suppose that he read the *Proslogion*. I claim here not a direct influence of Anselm of Canterbury on Dante the Florentine, only a fugitive affinity of imagination. This affinity extends to a few other writers, quite unconnected by the ordinary threads of 'influence'. The nearest in time to Dante is Guillaume de Lorris who wrote, less than a hundred years before the *Paradiso*, his allegorical *Roman de la rose*. De Lorris expressed the beginning and progress of a love affair through the image of a man wandering in a garden. The moment of falling in love is remarkable (I give the crucial passages from Chaucer's translation):

> And so befyl, I rested me
> Besydes a wel, under a tree . . .
> And on the border, al withoute,
> Was written in the ston aboute,
> Letters small, that sayden thus,
> 'Here starf[5] the fayre Narcisus' . . .
> Down at the botme set saw I
> Two cristall stonys craftely
> In thilke freshe and faire welle . . .
> For whanne the sonne, cler in sighte
> Cast in that well his bemys brighte,
> And that the heete descendid is,
> Thanne taketh the cristall stoon, ywis,
> Agayn the sonne an hundrid hewis,
> Blew, yelow, and red, that fresh and newe is,
> Yitt hath the merveilous cristall

[5] Starf = 'died'.

Such strengthe that the place overall,
Both flour, and tree, and leves grene,
And all the yerd in it is seene. . . .

In thilke mirrour saw I tho,
Among a thousand thinges mo,
A roser chargid full of rosis,
That with an hegge aboute enclos is.
Tho had I sich lust and envie,
That for Parys ne for Pavie
Nolde I have left to goon and see
There grettist hep of roses be.[6]

The moment when the man first sees his lady is the moment when he sees the roses. But he first sees the roses reflected in a crystal, lying at the bottom of a well of clear water where the sun's beams can still reach it. He knows at once (more swiftly than Dante) that what he saw reflected must exist in reality and therefore goes to look for the roses themselves. Moreover

This is the mirrour perilous,
In which the proude Narcisus
Saw all his face fair and bright. . . .

(1601–3)

In both passages we are deliberately reminded of Narcissus.

There is a kinship between Anselm, on the one hand, and Dante and de Lorris, on the other, but it would seem that the strange *logical* compulsion of the philosopher is to be found in neither poet. But here it is worth looking at two remoter analogues. First Shakespeare, in *Antony and Cleopatra*:

*Cleopatra*  For his bounty,
There was no winter in't; an autumn 'twas
That grew the more by reaping. His delights
Were dolphin-like: they show'd his back above
The element they liv'd in: in his livery
Walk'd crowns and crownets; realms and islands were
As plates dropp'd from his pocket.
*Dolabella*  Cleopatra —

<hr>

[6] Lines 1455–6, 1465–8, 1567–9, 1573–82, 1649–56; in *The Works of Geoffrey Chaucer*, ed. F. N. Robinson, 1957, pp. 579–80.

> *Cleopatra* Think you there was or might be such a man
>     As this I dreamt of?
> *Dolabella* Gentle Madam, no.
> *Cleopatra* You lie, up to the hearing of the gods.
>     But if there be nor ever were one such,
>     It's past the size of dreaming: nature wants stuff
>     To vie strange forms with fancy; yet t'imagine
>     An Antony were nature's piece 'gainst fancy,
>     Condemning shadows quite.
>
>                         (v. ii. 86–100)

Here, though the language is supremely lyrical, the context is
dialectical. Cleopatra, in a very strange manner, is arguing with
Dolabella. But it might be said that, although she is making a
(rather wilful) philosophical point, she is not making an exis-
tential point; instead of asserting that the Antony she loved
really existed, she so to speak weighs her image of Antony, with
all its richness and colour, against the grey tedium of the real
world and declares her preference for the image. But in the
words 'nature's piece 'gainst fancy' she ventures further;
indeed, she makes an existential point. Her argument is one
which should appeal strongly to the empiricist – not indeed to
the standard British empiricist of the eighteenth century and
afterward, whose concept of experience had been artificially
impoverished by the misapplication of scientific ideals (so that
only the measurable was truly 'real'), but the empiricist who is
willing to listen to and reverence real experience. Behind
Cleopatra's speech lies the suggestion that things are said to
exist according to the strength with which they are felt. Reality
is not established as a result of a successful check, in which the
sensory presentation is found to correspond exactly to the
reality, for the simple reason that creatures who have no organ
of perception but their senses have no chance to carry out such
a check. Reality is rather founded on the richness and stability
of the presentations themselves. And if this is the criterion,
Cleopatra implies, then the Antony of her love is more real (not
more 'real' but more real) than the rest of the world. Her voice
is shrill because she knows that one of the empirical criteria,
*intersubjective* availability, is not satisfied: Dolabella cannot

see what she sees. The reading 'nor' in line 96 in the first and second Folios well expresses a sort of momentary slippage of conviction. But she also speaks from a kind of confidence. She knows she has something of fundamental importance on her side.

My other analogue (still more remote from Dante in time) is Keats' account in his letter to Bailey of 22 November 1817 of the imagination:

> The Imagination may be compared to Adam's dream – he awoke and found it truth. I am the more zealous in this affair, because I have never yet been able to perceive how anything can be known for truth by consequitive reasoning – and yet it must be –[7]

Here, until the very last phrase, Keats' grip on the argument is firm. The good empiricist must always argue that nothing can be known for truth by consecutive reasoning *alone*. Valid conclusions can be drawn from true premisses, but in order to establish the truth of the premisses one will be driven at last to something which is merely given. On the other hand things *can* be known for true (the empiricist will maintain) on the basis of experience alone.

Thus Keats infers that there is after all no reason to reject the gifts of the imagination as unreal. To suppose a world without imagination is to suppose a world *substantially* impoverished. Before we even begin to ask whether an image is an image *of* an existent or a non-existent we must learn to ask, is the image itself a phenomenon? If the answer is yes, then it is part of the general fabric of reality.

Of course it remains true that while some images 'correspond to fact' (for example, the images of Canaletto or Vermeer) others (such as pictures of unicorns), do not. But the apparent absoluteness of this can be blurred in various ways. Once more we might insist that, strictly speaking, Canaletto does not correspond to an absolutely available, verifiable reality. There is rather a high degree of coherence between his

---

[7] In *The Letters of John Keats 1814–1821*, ed. H. E. Roltins, 1958, vol. 1, p. 185.

images and the intersubjectively available mass of impressions which has (quite properly) proved sufficiently stable over the years to yield us our ordinary language of material objects. Images of unicorns are at an opposite extreme. They do not correspond at all to the major web of intersubjective sense perception. Thus they can with justice be blamed, as compared with other images, for not being truth-tellers. They do not refer us to the major system. Note that this leaves their *intrinsic* phenomenal reality unimpaired. There really are images of unicorns in this world. It's just that these images do not do the *extra* job of pointing us to other patterns elsewhere.

But Keats was a Romantic, which means that his conception of imagination was certainly not confined either to passively representational imagery on the one hand or to purely fictive imagery on the other. We may see the world as a collection of material bodies or we may see it suffused with beauty and value. The second sort of perception Keats would think of as imaginative. Here his argument grows interesting. Fictive images like unicorns do not only fail to represent or refer to presentations available in the major system; they also fail to achieve the sort of relative stability and applicability to the objects of the major system which we find in words like 'grace' or 'goodness'. Though vivid they do not cohere sufficiently to produce even a secondary 'object language' (if for the moment we can think of the material of ethical discourse as a kind of set of objects). But ethical and aesthetic experience, as I have suggested, is another matter. Less 'hard' and stable than sense experience, it has nevertheless been stable enough to generate a language in which error and mendacity can be detected by language-users.

There is no better way to demonstrate this than simply to point to existing languages – to *any* existing language. The credit attaching to an ethical or aesthetic language is a little lower, epistemologically, than the credit attaching to sensory language, but it is fundamentally of the same order. It is not as if sense language carried an independent guarantee since, as we have seen, an independent check is impossible. In either case it is a matter of the greater or less stability of the images themselves.

We may also notice that society allows a certain credit even to the idiosyncratic 'perceptions' of lovers. A moment ago I observed that the Antony described by Cleopatra is not inter-subjectively available (though even that is a little too brusque: one suspects that it may have been partly available to Enobarbus). But even if we assume that it is visible to Cleopatra alone, this does not mean that it must lose any claim to the sort of coherence we have had in mind. For in the experience of a single subject an item may cohere, or not cohere with what precedes and follows it in time. When society sees an individual involved in such an idiosyncratically coherent experience of value, it does not consider that person either mad or deluded. It says, with a smile, perhaps, but often with fundamental respect, 'He (or she) is in love'. In fact, the argument put by Cleopatra amounts, if not to an ontological proof, at least to an ontological foray. To those who say 'You cannot get an existent out of an image' it answers 'You cannot get an existent any other way'.

That Shakespeare's thought could run on such lines is shown not only by Cleopatra's speech to Dolabella but also by Hippolyta's to Theseus. Theseus benevolently informs his bride that imagination is a tissue of lies. Hippolyta replies,

> But all the story of the night told over,
> And all their minds transfigured so together,
> More witnesseth than fancy's images,
> And grows to something of great constancy;
> But howsoever strange and admirable.
>
> (*A Midsummer Night's Dream*, v. i. 23–7)

Theseus is like John Locke, deluded by the hope of a guaranteed correspondence of perceptions to reality. Hippolyta is a better empiricist than either of them. She concedes at once that the night's wizardry does not correspond to the major object system, but is willing to see if it might not be strong enough to form its own object system. How did Theseus ever get his so comfortable world of fact (which let no man despise) unless from 'great constancy' of experiences?

Thus, if we grow accustomed to the idea that reality must be sought, not through some absolute external guarantee, but in the internal character of the material which presents itself to the mind, we shall find certain features of the Ontological Proof less shocking.

This reasoning turns out to have a force which transcends the limits of empiricism (of the authors I have considered here, Shakespeare and Keats are natural empiricists, Anselm, de Lorris and Dante are not). For example, the *axioms* of geometry are not known by 'consecutive reasoning' nor are they 'proved upon the pulses', exactly. Tell a mathematician that mathematics is an arbitrary human construct, and he will smile tolerantly and go and talk to someone else. He knows that mathematics is larger than he is. He knows that when he does mathematics he does not feign or construct things, but, more humbly, discovers them. I was once present at a discussion in which, after the philosophers had all stressed the fictive character of mathematics, the only mathematician present (and he a very good one) said, 'I'm afraid we mathematicians tend to be secret Platonists. It always seems like a process of discovery to us.'

Mathematicians know how that which from one point of view can seem 'merely conceptual', the deliberate product of an inventive human mind, can turn out to hold far more than any mind intentionally contributed to it. In this sense mathematics can soon begin to supply *objects* to our minds. It yields its own reality. Likewise with morality and even with aesthetic language. Philosophy since Locke has been dominated by the mistaken assumption that some external absolute check is necessary to any existential statement. Plato, who found his way to metaphysics from ethics and mathematics, worked differently. He worked like Anselm. In the *Phaedo* Plato advances one very curious argument for the immortality of the soul. He points out that certain qualities are *essential* to certain things; that is, if the quality is removed, the thing in question ceases to be itself and becomes some other thing. For example, coldness is essential to snow; heat up snow and it ceases to be snow. In like manner life is essential to soul (this is intuitively obvious to ancient Greeks, who habitually use the word for 'soul' to mean something like 'life-principle'). But, it may be objected, the fact that life is essential to soul does not mean that souls cannot be mortal; after all, if one can melt snow, why should not one be able to destroy a soul? Because, Plato answers, in the case of a quality like 'life' destruction is in direct contradiction to the quality ('Form') itself. Destruction is not logically incompatible with 'coldness', but it is incompatible with 'life'.[8] Thus the destruction of the soul is impossible. This argument is weird as Anselm's argument is weird. Indeed it is the same argument turned inside out. Where Anselm was proving the necessity of existence Plato is proving the impossibility of destruction. Plato assumes that what is *logically* precluded is *practically* impossible. Anselm assumes that the necessity of the concept is a necessity of fact.

It is no part of my intention to defend the logical cogency of Anselm's or of Plato's proof; my only purpose is to stress, in all the authors I have named, a common willingness to suppose that in some way or other facts may be constituted from a material which at first sight appears merely conceptual. Dante commits himself to this last, though he never commits himself to the detailed logic of Anselm.

As an interesting example, in our own time, of one occupying a middle position between the extremism of Anselm (or the Descartes of the Fifth *Meditation*) and ordinary scepticism we may take J. N. Findlay. In his essay, 'Can God's Existence be Disproved?'[9] Findlay concluded that while God does not exist in the ordinary sense of the term, it is perfectly proper to use the word *God* to denote the ideal focus of energies, aspirations and moral commitment. He writes, 'But there are other frames of mind, to which, we shouldn't deny the name "religious", which acquiesce quite readily in the non existence of their objects. (*This non-existence might, in fact, be taken to be the real meaning of saying that religious objects and realities are "not of this world"*)' (my italics).[10] That $\pi$ enables one to determine the area of a circle is a truth which seems likewise at no point to involve an 'existent' as Findlay understands the term. Yet it is certainly part of the fabric of the universe, and a

<hr>

[8] *Phaedo*, 102A–106E.
[9] In *New Essays in Philosophical Theology*, ed. A. Flew and A. MacIntyre, 1955, pp. 47–56.
[10] ibid., p. 56.

supra-personal, supra-cultural truth. There seems to be nothing to prevent God from being part of reality in the same or in an allied manner.

But there is an irony here. To echo Plato's reasoning, it is *essential* to the idea of God that he should be more than an idea, yet we seem to have been arguing that somehow the idea of him is enough. Not only must he be more than a mental conception; his substance must be stronger than that of mathematics. It is as if with God the notion of an utterly independent and absolute existence, which we have been concerned to get rid of, is an essential requirement. Anselm would eagerly intervene at this point to tell us that he had been saying just this all along, but I fear we cannot anticipate our results as he would have us do. If God is to be established as existing independently of all human concerns, the human feeling that he ought so to exist is not enough to ensure the result, and even the human discovery that he functions as a larger and more efficacious object of his thought than any individual could have foreseen is not enough to ensure the required supernatural independence.

Let us suppose that an evil God (say, Calvin's God plus a sense of humour) created this world. In time his creatures came, in their ignorance, to love him. Such a God might well laugh to see them worship him thus. But, equally, it might be said that the joke would be on God. For he would find himself excluded from something which, however it began, was now substantially greater than he. In G. K. Chesterton's *The Napoleon of Notting Hill* Auberon Quin confesses in the end to Adam Wayne that the whole idea of an army for Bayswater and a flag for Notting Hill began in his mind as a mere joke; Wayne answers that however it began it was also more than that; he joyously rejects the proffered disenchantment. One may well feel, after reading *The Napoleon of Notting Hill* that Quin's idea was neither funny nor heroic but merely unpleasant. But behind the strange conclusion of the book is a theological idea of some power. Before Quin confesses to Wayne he invites him to consider whether the creator might not know that the whole universe is really a joke. Wayne's reply is unanswerable: 'He could not know it, for it was not a joke.'

Chesterton thus applies the idea to the created world. But it can be turned, as I have suggested, back upon the creator. It might be said that a God of love who never created anything is greater than a loveless God who made everything. To reason thus is implicitly to ascribe substance to the ethical. But we must be willing to turn this sentence round also and grant that such 'substance' is only ethical and not practical. The God who made Heaven and Earth will never be reached by this path.

The ontological struggle to find the existence of God in the concept of God has been echoed in this book on the more trivial plane of content and authorship. We have insisted that certain assertions within a work naturally entail consequences for the author outside it: that if Herbert within a poem rejects literary convention he can be legitimately rebuked, as a man, for writing a poem at all. It seems obvious that our criticisms of Herbert and Milton are applicable to Dante. What could God have thought as He watched this man telling his peers all about Hell, Purgatory and Heaven, when he had not even died? What is God to think, when in *Paradiso* XXIV Dante has himself subjected to a brief examination by St Peter and awards himself a sort of upper second? As with Herbert and Milton the good faith of Dante could theoretically be saved if we could believe that the whole work were really the record of a mystical vision. But once again the length and the idiosyncratic human detail of the work makes such a suggestion incredible. As Stesichorus sang,

οὐκ ἔστ᾽ ἔτυμος λόγος οὗτος,
οὐδ᾽ ἔβας ἐν νηυσὶν εὐσέλμοις
οὐδ᾽ ἵκεο πέργαμα Τροίας.

It isn't true, this story. You never went on the well-benched ships, you never reached the towers of Troy.[11]

Yet of these three poets Dante, in his breath-taking inversion of the myth of Narcissus, comes nearest to breaking free of our objections. It is surely not extravagant to see in the figure of Narcissus a reference to the very problem of egoism which

[11] Quoted by Plato in *Phaedrus*, 243A (in *Poetae Melici Graeci*, ed. D. L. Page, 1962, p. 104).

has concerned us throughout the study (though to be sure we were concerned more with the literary implications while Dante is concerned with the moral). By invoking the figure of Narcissus Dante forestalls and deflects this criticism. This, in Herbert or Milton, would be my cue to write, 'Dante shows Dante mistaken and confused, which looks like humility, but what of the Dante who contrives the scene; is *he* humble?' As far as I can see, an answer may be simply, yes. For in showing us how the objects of the pilgrim's sight usurp and interrupt his own natural reactions, Dante may be hinting that, even though the poem may not be, literally, a vision of the world beyond, in entering upon it he found himself surprised by something far more active, far larger than the ordinary materials of literary art.

Certainly, he pursues his absurdly presumptuous topographical tour and continues blandly to invent the discourse of angels. But he does not tell us what the Father said to the Son or how the Spirit met his moral arguments. At the end he does not describe; he prays, and there is no reason why the prayer should not be a real prayer, existing indifferently inside and outside the poem. Beside the tender yet unresting humility of *Piers Plowman*, the *Commedia* will always seem brazen. But there remains a sense in which the world of the *Commedia*, as it grows to something of great constancy, transcends the very personality which so pungently pervades it. It is more than Dante. He never travelled through Hell, Purgatory and Paradise, but he really found another world.

# IV. CODA: ST JOHN'S
# GOSPEL

## I

## DISCONTINUOUS DIALOGUE

THIS STUDY began with George Herbert and with his habit of giving public, poetic form to God's answers to prayer. It seemed that as long as those answers were purely Scriptural we had no serious cause for disquiet. Our worries began when Herbert became inventive. But Herbert lived in the seventeenth century when belief in Scripture came more easily than it does today. What happens when a modern innocent turns his attention to the Bible, thinking it (for he knows no better) a book or set of books written by men about a person supposed divine? It is no longer *given* that the entire text is divine. Rather we have a situation in which a set of writings purporting to provide theological, moral and historical truth includes dialogue with the supposedly divine person. Does this mean that, in the very book which stood as a kind of rock in the discussion of Herbert, the Herbert paradox is in fact repeated – that Herbert in all good faith was leaning on men who had problems very like his own?

But first I propose a *Gedankenexperiment*. Let us read a passage of dialogue in John on the assumption that it is a piece of fiction, a work of literary art. Let us take Jesus's conversation with Pilate:

Then Pilate entered into the judgement hall again, and called Jesus, and said unto him, Art thou the King of the Jews? Jesus answered him, Sayest thou this thing of thyself, or did others tell it thee of me?

Pilate answered, Am I a Jew? Thine own nation and the chief priests have delivered thee unto me: what hast thou done? Jesus answered, My kingdom is not of this world. If my kingdom were of this world, then would my servants fight, that I should not be delivered to the Jews: but now is my kingdom not from hence.

Pilate therefore said unto him, Art thou a king then? Jesus answered, Thou sayest that I am a king. To this end was I born, and for this cause came I into the world, that I should bear witness unto the truth. Everyone that is of the truth heareth my voice.

And Pilate said unto him, What is truth?

(18: 33–8)

This is a remarkably early specimen of what literary critics call discontinuous dialogue. When Jesus is asked if he is king of the Jews, he answers neither yes or no but instead asks a question of his own. When he is asked what he has done, he answers not that question but the earlier one with the mysterious 'My kingdom is not of this world'. Even so, he skips one logical stage; to make the logic fully explicit he would presumably have had to say something like 'I am a king, yes, but not of the Jews nor of anything earthly'. This logical ellipse seems to trouble Pilate and he asks, seeking confirmation, 'Art thou a king, then?' and hears in answer the words 'Thou sayest that I am'.

Now the usual story told by scholars of drama is that the discontinuous dialogue in favour with the *epigoni* of Harold Pinter really began with Chekhov. Chekhovian dialogue sounds like this:

*Liubov Andreyeevna* How you've aged, Feers!
*Feers* What can I get you, Madam?
*Lopahin* They say, you've aged a lot.
*Feers* I've been alive a long time. They were going to marry me off before your Dad was born. (*Laughs*) And when

Freedom was granted to the people, I'd already been made the chief valet. I wouldn't take my Freedom then, I stayed with the master and mistress. ... (*Pause*) I remember everyone was glad at the time, but what they were glad about, no one knew.

*Lopahin* Oh yes, it was a good life all right. At least, people got flogged!

*Feers* (*not having heard him*) Rather! The peasants belonged to the gentry, and the gentry belonged to the peasants; but now everything's separate, and you can't understand anything.[1]

Again, notice the systematic absence of 'logical fit'. Of course the literary critics allow that although Chekhov is for practical purposes the *fons et origo* of this manner, it is always on the cards that Shakespeare, who could do anything, did this. And indeed he did. Here is a passage from the second part of *Henry IV*:

*Shallow* By the mass, I could anger her to th' heart. She was then a *bona roba*. Doth she hold her own well?

*Falstaff* Old, old, Master Shallow.

*Shallow* Nay, she must be old, she cannot choose but be old, certain's she's old, and had Robin Nightwork by old Nightwork before I came to Clement's Inn.

*Silence* That's fifty-five years ago.

*Shallow* Ha, cousin Silence, that thou hadst seen that that this knight and I have seen? Ha, Sir John, said I well?

*Falstaff* We have heard the chimes at midnight, Master Shallow.

(III. ii. 199–210)

Thus far back and no further. By and large, it takes a modernist to relish discontinuity, to rejoice more in silence than in palpable structure, and Shakespeare is merely (as so often) the exception that proves the rule. Elsewhere as far as the eye can see lie tracts of *connected* writing.

So what are we to make of the Gospel? Is it a freakish anticipation of modernism? A very little thought suggests that

[1] *The Cherry Orchard*, Act II, in *Plays*, trans. Elisaveta Fen, 1959, pp. 361–2.

it is not. The principle of discontinuity which holds in both Shakespeare and Chekhov is quite different from that which holds in the Gospel. The world of Shakespeare's Gloucester-shire scenes and Chekhov's Cherry Orchard is in a manner one place: a world of ill-disciplined servants, ill-managed material circumstances and asthenic yet poignant emotions. Here dialogue is above all desultory; discontinuities occur not only between speeches but in the middle of speeches, showing that the characters are not only failing to communicate but as individuals lack coherent, autonomous drive. Madam Liubov's orchard, Justice Shallow's orchard; both are symbols of a sort of sweet-smelling death. But in the oblique answers of Jesus we sense rather an awful life.

The dialogue with Pilate may be discontinuous, then, but it is anything but desultory. We are not made to watch people drifting away from each other and themselves into a kind of reminiscent vacuum, but rather disputants locked in combat. The discontinuities of Jesus (and of Pilate – for he begins to learn the game) are evidently deliberate. They are at the very lowest a way of holding the initiative at all times. Answer a man directly and you are playing his game, dancing to his tune. A constitutional inability to answer a straight question seems to have marked out Jesus from the first. The people looked for him and at last found him in Capernaum (6: 25) and asked him when he had arrived there, which is a simple enough question. Jesus does not say 'Yesterday' or anything resembling that. He says, 'Ye seek me, not because ye saw the miracles but because ye did eat of the loaves and were filled.' That is, he immediately assumes the initiative and overrides them. When later the Jews ask (8: 19) 'Where is thy father?' he answers (*answers?*) 'Ye neither know me nor my father: if ye had known me ye had known my father also.' Here we begin to see more clearly that together with a seizing of the initiative there is further a technique of deliberate transcendence. Jesus's (non-) answer implies that their assumptions in asking the question were all wrong, that they were thinking on the wrong plane. Yet, note, he could have told them this and yet preserved the form of a direct answer; that is, he could have said, 'In Heaven'. But of course such an answer would not have quickened the minds of his listeners anything like as effectively as the answer he chose. Which perhaps is as much as to say, he chose to express his transcending answer in a form obfuscated for rhetorical purposes. Later in the same chapter (7: 25) he is asked, 'Who art thou?' and answers, 'Even the same that I said unto you from the beginning.' This could of course be a perfectly normal exasperated response, except for the fact that Jesus has not as far as we know been telling anyone in any straightforward sense who he is from the beginning. Nor need we postulate a *lacuna* in the text, for we are told that the Jews themselves found his answer unintelligible. So we must place this answer in the same category as the others. It too is a transcending non-answer. Later in the same dialogue Jesus says to the Jews (8: 5) 'Your father Abraham rejoiced to see my day' and they not unnaturally react: 'Thou art not yet fifty years old, and hast thou seen Abraham?' Jesus answers (and here 'lack of logical fit' seems too weak a description) 'Before Abraham was, I am.'

Nor is it only with outsiders that Jesus speaks thus. Simon Peter said to him (13: 6) 'Lord, dost thou wash my feet?' and Jesus said, 'What I do thou knowest not now, but thou shalt know hereafter.' Obviously in this last example it would be absurd in any sort of discourse to give the formally apposite answer, 'Yes, I am washing your feet.' Clearly Simon Peter is not querying the fact, but the propriety of the fact. He means, 'You're surely not going to wash my feet, are you?' But, equally obviously, Jesus might have begun his answer by saying, 'Yes, I am indeed going to do this.' But he prefers a baffling ellipsis and a statement which transcends the merely social morality of Simon Peter's question.

Looked at coldly this technique of arrogant obliqueness, once analysed, can appear singularly infuriating. The basic mechanism is surprisingly simple, and it is easy to turn out such dialogue by the yard. For example:

*White* Are you going to the Conference on Friday?
*Black* Am I? Persuade me.
*White* Gombrich will be there.
*Black* If you like Gombrich, that is the sort of thing you like.

*White*  Why, don't you like Gombrich?
*Black*  Let's say that I don't.

To write such dialogue is a curious experience (now I testify)
partly because one senses a powerful latent evil in the smiling,
quizzical answers of Black. One thinks wildly for a moment
that the whole story of Christ is latent in his mere style; people
who talk in this way, one feels, are liable to be crucified (or
made to drink hemlock). But while the gaps in modernist
dialogue imply a kind of anti-nature, the gaps in Jesus's
dialogue imply a transcending complement, a super-nature.

I have suggested that there is no analogue earlier than the
Gloucestershire scenes of Shakespeare's *Henry IV* for the dis-
continuous dialogue of the Gospels and that even that example
was in truth scarcely analogous. Certainly the dialogue of even
the most mysterious Greek tragedies – *Oedipus Coloneus* for
example or the *Bacchae* – seems pellucidly consecutive beside
the dialogue of John's Gospel. The non-answers given by the
Delphic Oracle are perhaps to some extent comparable. These
responses, however, do not in practice intimate substantial
transcendent verities, but prudently ambiguous practical pre-
dictions. The hieratic ambiguity has an evident function. Mor-
ton Smith has described a tradition of Delphic Secrecy in
sectarian Jewish religion at the time of Jesus and seems at one
point to assign a similarly prudent motive to the Jewish prac-
tice.[2] The followers of Christ may have been in some respects
libertine and it was merely wise to keep such goings-on hidden.
But this explanation scarcely covers the words of Jesus as we
have them. Jesus seems less concerned with concealment than
with some shocking revelation. There seems to be a Northern
tradition of responses at once dour and equivocal, at least as
old as the Sagas and at least as young as R. L. Stevenson, which
makes some faint approach, but it is faint indeed. But half a
page ago I mentioned hemlock; does the example of Socrates
shed any light? The Platonic dialogues, considered as a drama-
tic form, are at first sight far too consecutive. Paradoxically, it

[2] *The Secret Gospel: The Discovery and Interpretation of the Secret Gospel
According to Mark*, New York, 1973.

is rather in the *Apology* – a monologue – that we find a kind of parallel to the utterance of Jesus. After all, the whole of the *Apology* is a kind of answer and a non-answer to a series of questions. Did Socrates corrupt the young? He answers, 'Would a man wish to make his fellows better or worse?' (transposing the discussion to the *a priori*). What punishment did he deserve? He answers, 'Maintenance free of charge in the Prytaneum' (rejecting the very notion of punishment).[3] And all the while, amid the wreckage of his conventional legal defence, we sense an enormous mystery.

The excuse of Socrates for his appalling incivility was that he had seen something incommensurate with the world he inhabited. The way Plato put it was that he had apprehended the Ideas which exist beyond the sensible world, but this is probably already too definite. The excuse of Herbert was essentially the same; he had heard a voice from beyond humanity, or if he had not, he blasphemed his own law. The Evangelist's situation seems to be essentially similar.

John says at the beginning of his Gospel that the Word which *was* God was made flesh and dwelt among us. He makes it plain that this incarnate God is to be identified with Jesus, that Jesus made the world, entered it and was rejected by it, that Jesus was 'the true light, that lighteth every man that cometh into the world' (1: 9). This Jesus, then, was more than man. But within a page this divine man is speaking, and we need urgently to know: are the words Jesus's own or are they John's (for John was only a man)? If we choose the first interpretation, or indeed a modified version of it whereby the words of Jesus could have been believed by John to have been Jesus's own, our course is easy. But if we choose the second, and suppose that John is in any degree ingeniously constructing this transcending dialogue of Jesus, then at once the Herbert problem confronts us. It might be thought that we do not have that special irony we find in Herbert, whereby a kind of moral solipsism in the praying subject is presented in such terms as to make it clear that only a voice from outside can resolve it, a voice from outside is then seemingly produced but turns out after all to be

---

[3] 25A–26A, 36D.

fiction of the benighted subject. In John the problem assumes a different and more universal form. It is the world, not the author on his knees, that is the benighted subject, and that night is presented in such a way as to make clear that only the intervention of superhuman power can dispel it. Not even an exceptional man like John the Baptist can give true light (1: 8–9), only the supernatural can irradiate the natural. But, we are told, this indeed happened and the Evangelist can tell us the superhuman words of the superhuman man. But if John, natural man, to any considerable extent concocted those words *for* Christ, both his argument and his good faith are in ruins. Only the superhuman will serve, and the superhuman is the one thing which natural man, however pious and willing, cannot undertake to provide.

But now we begin to see that the contrast between Herbert as contending with moral solipsism and John as contending with naturalism is partly unsatisfactory. The similarity, in fact, is stronger than the difference. The praying Herbert within the poem fails, not because he is cut off from moral contact with his fellow creatures, but simply *quā* creature: he fails because he is not God, and this is equally true of every other human being. Thus, Herbert's predicament within the poem is implicitly universal, and moreover the universal situation turns out to be identical with that proposed by John. And so the distance between them shrinks. What we took for a distant analogy is something a good deal closer than that. At the same time, however, the word 'solipsism' retains a certain paradoxical appropriateness. The solipsist trembles lest all outside himself should prove an illusion, leaving him, as Hume said, 'environed with darkness'. The Christian trembles lest all outside humanity and nature should prove an illusion, leaving his entire species benighted. The phrase 'collective solipsism' or 'solipsism of the species' may seem contradictory, but the religious mind instantly endows it with a perfectly coherent meaning. Even the etymological element represented by *sol* in *solipsism*, the element of alone-ness, persists in the collective version, since now the fear is that if the human race is in no sort of relation with the transcendent, then the entire race is horribly alone. The kind of moral solipsism which Herbert wrestles with in his poems is really – for all his interest in the individual praying by himself – collective solipsism.

Solipsism, once it is permitted to pose itself as a problem, can only be cured from outside. Self-comforting fictions produced by the suffering subject will not serve, precisely because they are produced by the subject. This reasoning applies indifferently to individual and to collective solipsism. 'External' cure in the case of the individual solipsist means cure from a person or thing other than himself. 'External' cure for the collective religious solipsist consists in cure from a being who does not belong to the human race or the natural order. Christianity differs from most if not all religions in recognizing this necessity and supplying, through the Incarnation, the required external cure.

But now I must draw a distinction. I said earlier that even when Herbert draws his divine replies from a live tradition, he remains at fault in so far as his dramatic resolution depends on an *actual* reply from God; what is most dramatically effective in the poems is the fact that the man praying actually *hears* (however faintly) the voice of one saying 'Child' so that external cure appears in exactly the way most urgently required – but then this turns out to be fiction. By parity of reasoning we must seemingly allow that the Evangelist is in better case. For even if the *content* of Jesus's speeches were feigned by him, we need not suppose (need we?) that he doubted the *fact* of Jesus's appearance on earth. *That* he spoke is as important as *what* he spoke.

Here my argument begins to see-saw uncomfortably: lose Herbert, save John, lose John, save Herbert. Thus, in the second section of the first part of this book, I suggested that the *fact* of an audible reply to prayer is not the only external cure recognized by the Christian. Indeed the antithesis between fact and content is in one respect highly misleading. 'The very nature of Jesus's moral and spiritual teaching proclaims it Other than the world, and this *fact* about *content* supplies an adequate corrective to the merely human.' To think thus is to make just such an ontological move from idea to fact as we discussed in the last chapter. According to this reasoning, the fiction whereby Herbert has God speak at the end of the poem becomes a venial fiction, since it is no longer on the *fact* of a reply that the very existence of an external correction depends. But if we apply this reasoning to the Gospel and suppose that the Evangelist supplied part of the *doctrine* of the Gospel, since it is now *doctrine* which most crucially supplies the necessary correction of the merely human, then the good faith of the Evangelist is in serious jeopardy. Conversely, as we have seen, if the mere fact that God has appeared and spoken is crucial, then Herbert is in trouble and the Evangelist is safe.

It is by now obvious that I have run up against questions of fact and probability. The question: 'Is the Jesus of John's Gospel a construction of the Evangelist, a construction of tradition or Jesus himself?' is of course a question for scholars. Such faint echoes of controversy as reach my ears suggest that the most extreme view, namely that the Evangelist has largely constructed Jesus for us, is by no means out of court. But I make no pronouncement. I confine myself to deductions from theoretical possibilities.

Thus, if we absolve the Evangelist of employing any art in the matter, all our problems fasten with redoubled force, on Jesus himself. For Jesus did not claim to have heard the divine voice. He claimed to be the divine voice. This is the highest point in an escalating series of difficulties, and here we find no resolution, but rather a knot drawn tight.

So our contrast between the 'feigned-audible' answer of God in Herbert and the less contentious physical availability of Jesus begins to lose its urgency as it is replaced by a more importunate doubt. Everything now depends on the nature of the Jesus who was thus available. Was he man or was he God? We are driven to concentrate no longer upon the physical availability of a certain body, but rather upon the veracity of a certain claim.

I have deliberately delayed discussion of the most tantalizing of all Jesus's answers to Pilate: 'Thou sayest that I am.' We may distinguish three kinds of equivocal answer. The first is merely evasive, the second obliquely adumbrates a universe of discourse which transcends the assumptions of the original question, and the third directs attention to a realm which is *radically* transcendent, so utterly Other as to resist any kind of specific illustration in human terms. Jesus is a king but has nothing specific in common with other kinds. In what way, then, is he a king? One is driven back on a kind of tautology; he shares with other kings the property of sovereignty or rule. So Pilate repeats the question, 'Art thou a king, then?' And Jesus uses in reply an idiom which at one level implies simple assent, but at another more formal level merely bounces the question back (the Authorized Version is carefully literal at this point): 'Thou sayest that I am.' Even if it were shown that in Aramaic the idiom 'thou sayest', like the American 'You've said it', was regularly used as an affirmative, so that Jesus is committing himself to rather more than, '"King" is your word for it', in a situation as tense as this one would suspect that the speaker might nevertheless be taking refuge in the literal meaning of the words. Imagine a man being interrogated during the McCarthy investigations:

'Are you or have you at any time ever been a Communist?'

'You've said it.'

In such circumstances such a reply would immediately sound uneasily equivocal and I have little doubt that the Senator from Wisconsin would press for a less ambiguous answer. Thus, even if Jesus may be said to have assented to Pilate's question (and even that is doubtful) he does so in an idiom which at another level merely retorts the question back upon Pilate; moreover his choice of this idiom is probably not accidental. He answers, but in another way he merely echoes, and the mystery lies somewhere between the assent and the echo, no longer to be specifically hinted. George Herbert wrote a poem in which Heaven answered him in an echo only, but an echo which was at the same time miraculously informative:

O who will show me those delights on high?
*Echo* I.

Thou, Echo, thou art mortall, all men know.
*Echo* No.

This will serve as an emblem of what happens in Jesus's dialogue with Pilate, but it is an emblem only, and not a strict parallel. In the poem the blankness of the echo is almost too easily defeated by the little miracle of literary ingenuity; each repetition is made into a perfectly meaningful and intelligible answer. But in Jesus's answer to Pilate the element of blank intransigence is less easily dispelled.

## II

## EITHER/OR

I HAVE argued that the discontinuous answers of Jesus are virtually unique and that this uniqueness requires a special explanation. My own response has been that the hiatus between question and answer arises from the extraordinary, other-worldly character of the answers. Behind 'Thou sayest that I am' stands nothing less than 'I am God'. Under such pressures the ordinary fabric of discourse gives way. At the same time, however, Jesus's words have a stylistic context, which I take to be one of immemorial Jewish irony. This irony is hard to describe but, once noticed, easily recognized. Oddly enough, there is a touch of it in Pilate's 'Am I a Jew?' (was the Roman governor going native?). The *Talmud* might be described as in part a book of entirely pious jokes about God. Here, if you like, is a real analogue to what Jesus is doing. But the effect of this discovery is not to remove the uniqueness of Jesus' language but to emphasize it. True, in both cases the irony often arises from the baffling gap between human and divine, but in the *Talmud* the human speakers, merchants, rabbis, all are merely human and God is other than they. Jesus alters the very grammar of Talmudic humour, applies it in the first person singular and assumes a position in the joke which no one had presumed to occupy before (unless it was Lucifer).

But now further differences between Herbert and John begin to press upon us. My argument against Herbert is largely *ad hominem*. That is, when I am asked by what absurd ideal of literalness in language and unquestioning humility in man I censure Herbert, I answer, the ideals are Herbert's own. The England of Elizabeth had been predominantly Calvinist, and the England of Herbert's time was still powerfully Puritan in its theology. It was not I but the author of *Jordan I* and *II* who affirmed that only the plainest truth would do for devotion. It was not I but a theology still potent in Herbert's time which affirmed that the very effort to deserve the love of God was itself a kind of pride. But how much of this applies to John? I have suggested that nothing less than the *ipsissima verba* of the divine man will do, but John may not have had even the concept of accurate verbatim quotation. At least, it is a pretty safe rule that no Ancient ever quotes another accurately. Plato's quotations from Homer are always perfectly metrical, perfectly Homeric but rarely if ever impeccable. And, as I observed earlier, Plato was willing to attribute to his dead teacher philosophical views he never held.

Perhaps, then, John never asked himself point-blank whether Jesus really said x or y but contented himself with writing down only what seemed 'right', or harmonious with memory and tradition. Does this mean that the *ad hominem* charge of mendacity cannot be put? I answer, the problem has assumed an altogether starker form and will not go away. If John is in bad faith it will not be because he has like Herbert personally supplied the words which God might have said but rather because he has pretended *simpliciter* that Jesus was God; likewise, if John was honest, his honesty does not consist in the accurate transmission of words duly vouchsafed to him, but rather in the truthful recounting of the most extraordinary of all *facts*. You do not need a puritan theology or a scholarly training to know the difference between explaining how Jesus was God, and pretending that Jesus was God. In any case, if my argument is not *ad hominem*, it is *ad deum ipsum*. It scarcely matters that Puritanism with its emphasis on plain truth has not yet emerged, since what is now in question is not the accurate tradition of a transcendent truth or the propriety of such discourse under God, but the original self-declaration of God, if God it was. Let us take it step by step.

First, let us suppose that John, for political or missionary reasons, produced the claim to be divine on Jesus' behalf. That is hideous bad faith. In a Greek or Roman of the period it might have merited a milder description. After all, the classical world at that time abounded in θεῖοι ἄνδρες, 'divine men', – so much so that the word *divine* meant little more than 'charismatic', and I deliberately choose a debased English word. But John was a Jew, and Jews, however well informed about Greek philosophy, had an altogether heavier conception of deity. The Word, the Logos, is taken from the Greeks but in no docile spirit, for it is instantly *made flesh*, a most un-Greek conception. In a famous passage in the *Confessions* Augustine says how he read in the Platonists of the divine Word, 'but that the Word was made flesh and dwelt among us I did not read there' (7: 9). John was no crypto-Hellene. He knew that to describe a Jew as calling himself God was not in the least like referring to the self-deification of an Emperor. Here, if you like, is the equivalent moment to my appeal to Puritanism in connection with Herbert. At the very least, the Jewish conception of deity is Puritan, while the Graeco-Roman conception is cavalier (in the pejorative sense of the word).

Second, let us suppose instead that John was repeating, in good faith, a tradition about Jesus which he believed to be true. In this case we can bring no charge against John. Instead we must interrogate (theoretically of course since it is in practice impossible) the earlier transmitters of the story. And, at every stage, either the teller is inventing the claim to be divine (and that is hideous bad faith) or else he is repeating what he believes to be true – until we come at last to the historical Jesus. One might suppose the story to have grown by insensible degrees, but the supposition is not easy. Even if we assume that at an earlier stage Jesus claimed divine parentage and no more, and this was inflated through mis-hearing and the unconscious distortions of memory, the original claim is, in a Jewish context, sufficiently stark. It is an assertion of the intersection of the transcendent with the natural. Somewhere, some such claim must have been introduced. And always it must have been clear that it was either an awful lie or a more awful truth.

Lying behind a great deal of what I have said is the old, fierce alternative *aut deus aut malus homo*, 'either God or a wicked man'. But in truth there is one other possibility, and that is that

Jesus was mad. After long hesitation I find that this explanation, initially so repulsive, is the one I think most likely to be true. After all, I write, not as an Evangelical Christian, but as one brought up by unbelieving parents in an unbelieving culture, true to that nurture and that culture by mature conviction, and yet, with all this, exasperated by the enervate professions of believers. It is as if one's very scepticism is somehow dishonoured when it finds itself confronted by such half-belief. When I say that Jesus may have been mad I am working on the assumption that the possibilities of natural explanation should be exhausted before supernatural explanation is invoked. The natural explanation turns out to be a less simple affair than it seemed. The supposition that Jesus was wicked is of course in immediate difficulties. To many people the supposition of madness will be equally difficult. But this reaction rises in part, I suspect, from two false presumptions: first, that madness is the opposite of intelligence and second that madness is incompatible with goodness. In fact, most dull-witted people are sane and many mad people are luminously intelligent. Some mad people, likewise, have more than the common allowance of charity. There have been many mad men who thought they were God. The special irony with Jesus is that, so far from being a case of megalomania compensating for utter incapacity, his real claim upon our reverence is immense. The emperor Caligula thought he ruled the universe and really ruled the known world. Jesus thought he was God and was really the best of men.

The last chapter of this book is essentially a plea to people to see what a knife-edge thing the Gospel of John is. Modern readers seem to have acquired some way of talking about Scripture which somehow absolves them from the need to notice the one extraordinary thing that Scripture says, as if they do not, in these sophisticated times, need to make any sort of decision on the point. Perhaps they have all gently agreed (clerics and laymen, all) that Jesus was somewhat deranged and told lies. This, as I have confessed, is my own provisional position. It still dismays me that they take up this position with such complaisant equanimity, with no more, so to speak, than a nod and a wink across the board-room table – as if this were the least of the questions that confronted them. It is, at the lowest, bad literary criticism (like discussing *Romeo and Juliet* without once acknowledging that the play is about love). This barbarous reader took no belief to his reading of the Gospel. But the first thing he encountered was a frontal challenge to that unbelief.

# INDEX